THE CIVIL WAR DIARY OF
LIEUTENANT ROBERT MOLFORD ADDISON
Co. E, 23rd Wisconsin Infantry
December 24, 1863–December 29, 1864

Edited by
Diane E. Greene, AG

HERITAGE BOOKS
2014

HERITAGE BOOKS
AN IMPRINT OF HERITAGE BOOKS, INC.

Books, CDs, and more—Worldwide

For our listing of thousands of titles see our website at
www.HeritageBooks.com

Published 2014 by
HERITAGE BOOKS, INC.
Publishing Division
5810 Ruatan Street
Berwyn Heights, Md. 20740

Copyright © 2001 Diane E. Greene

Heritage Books by the author:

Boulder City Cemetery, Boulder City, Clark County, Nevada, 1942 to June 2000 Volumes 1 and 3

Mary Eliza Easton Diary, Loudon, Franklin County, Pennsylvania

Nevada Civil War Claims: Legislative Reports, 1888–1900

The Civil War Diary of Lieutenant Robert Molford Addison, Co. E, 23rd Wisconsin Volunteer Infantry, December 24, 1863–December 29, 1864

All rights reserved. No part of this book may be reproduced or transmitted in any form or by any means, electronic or mechanical, including photocopying, recording or by any information storage and retrieval system without written permission from the author, except for the inclusion of brief quotations in a review.

International Standard Book Numbers
Paperbound: 978-1-58549-656-3
Clothbound: 978-0-7884-6015-9

Contents

Introduction.................................... v.

Background

    Robert M. Addison - family...................... 1

    Wisconsin Twenty-third Infantry................. 9

    Battles... 11

    The Mississippi River Fleet..................... 13

Civil War Diary.................................. 15

Friends and Acquaintances......................... 103

Suggestions for Further Reading................... 175

Index.. 179

Introduction

Approximately 12,000 Union troops fought in the April 1864 battles of Sabine Cross Roads and Pleasant Hill in Louisiana. The diary of Lieutenant Robert M. Addison, Company E, Twenty-third Wisconsin Infantry, covers December 1863 through 1864, discussing these battles and the Red River Campaign that followed. The purpose of this work is to let the words of Addison describe what was going on in his world and, through annotation of his diary (in boldface) to put his experiences into perspective with what others were doing during that time. The purpose was to also learn about the men mentioned in the diary. What were their experiences during the war? What were their lives like after the war?

The Twenty-third Wisconsin had an original strength of 994 men, but only 416 mustered out. Of those men, Addison mentioned fifty-five in the diary. The basic information on these men in the section "Friends and Acquaintances" was gleaned from the regimental descriptive rolls and service and pension records in the National Archives. The first part of these biographies includes birth information and the men's war experiences. The second part describes their family life and postwar experiences. County histories, obituaries, and various other sources were consulted to compile information on Addison's friends and acquaintances.

The War of the Rebellion: A Compilation of the Official Records of the Union and Confederate Armies, regimental histories, and *Compiled Records Showing Military Service of Military Units in Volunteer Union Organizations of Wisconsin* were the foundation of the annotations to the diary. Also included are signatures, photographs, and Addison family information. A sample page of the diary is included, as is a list of suggestions for further research.

The original diary is at the State Historical Society of Wisconsin, 816 State Street, Madison, Wisconsin. It was donated 15 January 1872 by Mrs. Robert Molford Addison of Oberlin, Ohio, whose husband was a grandson of Lt. Addison. Robert M. Addison a second great-grand uncle of the editor, Diane E. Greene.

I would like to thank my friends and colleagues for their suggestions and moral support to this project. Special thanks to Ken Nelson, AG, Steven B. Rhodes, and Marie Varrelman Melchiori, CGRS, for their guidance regarding military records. I would also like to thank Carol Ekdahl, AG, Pam Peterson; Beverly Rice, CGRS, Glen Roosevelt, and Gordon Remington, FASG, and Roger Joslyn, CG, FASG.

Background: Robert Addison Family

Robert Molford Addison was born on 12 June 1840, in Manchester, Lancashire, England, the son of Dr. Robert Addison and Harriet Hodson. The following is a summary of the immediate family.

DR. ROBERT ADDISON

Robert Addison was born 8 March 1803. He was christened on 18 March 1803 in Frodsham, Chester, England, the son of John and Esther Addison. He died on 2 October 1876 in Waseca, Waseca County, Minnesota and was buried on 6 October 1876 in Mazomanie Cemetery, Mazomanie, Dane County, Wisconsin.

Dr. Robert Addison qualified as a doctor in 1829 and in 1831. He was an apprentice to Mr. George Preston of Warrington. His home at the time of his enlistment in the Civil war, was Mazomanie. He served as First Assistant Surgeon of the 19th Wisconsin Infantry from 30 August 1862 until 3 March 1863. They released him from service because he was "too feeble to continue to serve." [1]

He married Harriet Hodson (daughter of John Hodson and Ann Lee) on 27 September 1834 in Manchester, Lancashire, England. **Harriet Hodson** was born on 22 September 1813 in Manchester and was christened on 14 October 1813 in St. John's, Manchester. She died on 21 September 1863 in Arena, Iowa County, Wisconsin and was buried in the Mazomanie Cemetery.[2]

They had the following children:

---

[1] Letter dated 14 Sep 1989, from Guildhall Library, Aldermanbury, London. S. Freeth, Keeper of Manuscripts. Information extracted from Guildhall Library MS.8241/S, *The Candidates Qualification Entry Book, 1829-1832*, of the Society of Apothecaries; *County of Chester, Frodsham Parish Church (St. Lawrence) Registers, Baptisms 1558-1812 (*Worchester: Ebenr. Baylis & Son, 1913), 1: 552; Dr. Robert Addison Obituary, *Mazomanie Sickle*, October 1876; Mazomanie Cemetery records. Mazomanie, Dane, Wisconsin, Block 1, Lot 79; Dr. Robert Addison- Military Record, letter from Colonel Charles R. Gill Command 29th Regt. Wisconsin Infantry, Camp at Helena Arkansas February 16th, 1863.

[2] *Church of England. Cathedral Church (Manchester) Manchester, Lancaster, England. Parish registers, marriages 1834-1835*, p.150, No. 2245; *St. Johns Register of Manchester Baptisms 1813-1829*. Book 2:3.

2   Robert M. Addison: Civil War Diary

i.   **Harriet Matilda Addison** was born on 6 August 1835, christened on 9 September, in Manchester. She died on 6 July 1916, buried in Mazomanie. She married **Job Wilkinson** on 8 January 1856 in Arena. He was born 1832 in England and died on 3 January 1893, buried in the Mazomanie Cemetery.³

ii. **Emily Robertine Addison** was born on 10 February 1837 and christened on 22 June in Manchester. She died on 7 May 1894, buried in the Mazomanie Cemetery. She married **Walter Wilkinson** on 17 June 1864 in Iowa County.⁴

iii. **Ann Marie Addison** was born on 30 September 1838, christened on 21 June 1839 in Manchester. She died on 28 April 1934 in Spring Green, Sauk County, Wisconsin, buried on 1 May 1934 in the Arena Cemetery. She married **James Edward Ward** (son of William Allen Ward and Elizabeth Ried) on 5 May 1864 in Iowa County. He was born on 22 November 1838 in Kent, Nova Scotia, Canada. He died on 2 December 1910 in Arena, buried on 5 December 1910 in the Arena Cemetery.⁵

iv. **Robert Molford Addison** was born on 12 June 1840 in Manchester, England. He died on 11 April 1915 in Marshall, Lyon County, Minnesota. He married **Ella Amelia Wood** on 6 February 1868 in Waseca, Minnesota. She was born 1845 in St. Lawrence, New York, died on 25 January 1908 in Marshall, buried in the Marshall Cemetery.⁶

v.   **Amelia Stuart Addison** was born on 22 March 1843 in England. She died on 2 February 1917 in California. She married

---

³ *Church of England. Cathedral Church (Manchester) Manchester, Lancaster, England. Parish registers, baptisms.1833-1835.* p.507, No. 4049; Mazomanie Cemetery records. Mazomanie, Dane,Wisconsin, Block 1, Lot 78; Iowa County, Wisconsin Marriage 1: 272 #2594.

⁴ *Church of England. Cathedral Church (Manchester) Manchester, Lancaster, England. Parish registers, baptisms.1836-1838*, p. 429, No. 3427; Iowa County, Wisconsin Marriage 1: 388 # 274.

⁵ Manchester Cathedral Parish Records, Lancaster, England Christenings p. 304, No. 2432; Certificate of Death, Registered No. 2; Iowa County, Wisconsin Marriage 3: 297; Death Record, p. 756.

⁶ Civil War Pension File, Robert M. Addison, application #1096678, certificate #1106045; Mrs. R. M. Addison Obituary, *Lyon County Reporter*, 22 January 1908.

Background: Robert Addison Family   3

William Everett on 29 October 1865 in Arena, Wisconsin. He was born on 6 July 1828 in Sussex, New Jersey. He died on 16 June 1892 in California.[7]

vi.   **Evelina L. Addison** was born August 1845 in Rhode Island, died 21 June 1949.[8]

vii.   **Eliza H. Addison** was born August 1847 in Rhode Island. She died April 1851.[9]

viii.   **George F. Addison** was born December 1849 in Dover, Wisconsin. He died 29 October 1853 and was buried in Mazomanie Cemetery.

iv.   **Stanley H. Addison** was born 9 January 1853 in Dover. He died 28 September 1925 in Watertown, Clark County, South Dakota. He was married to **Adalade**, who was born in 1855 in New York.[10]

x.   **Clarence Albert Addison** was born 4 August 1855 in Dover, Wisconsin. He died 9 December 1939 in Colorado Spring, El Paso County, Colorado. He was buried on 11 December 1939 in Evergreen Cemetery, Colorado Springs. He married **Mary P.**[11]

xi.   **Albert C. Addison** was born 7 January 1859 in Dover, Wisconsin. He died 11 February 1930.

xii.   **Lillie H. Addison**, died 1861, buried in Mazomanie Cemetery.[12]

---

[7] Iowa County, Wisconsin Marriage, 1:409 # 400; James Erwin Child. *Child's History of Waseca County, Minnesota: From Its First Settlement in 1854 to the Close of the Year 1904. A Record of Fifty Years. The Story of the Pioneers.* (Tucson, Ariz,: W. C. Cox, Co., 1974), 704.
[8] Sara Evelyn Ward Thompson Eldert, personal papers.
[9] Sara Evelyn Ward Thompson Eldert, personal papers.
[10] S. H. Addison Obituary, *Daily Public Opinion,* Watertown, South Dakota, 29 September 1925, p.2; 1880 US Census, Lake Marshall, Marshall, Lyon, MN ed.144, st.5, line 39 45/46.
[11] Clarence A. Addison Obituary, *Sunday Gazette and Telegraph,* Colorado Springs, Colorado, 10 December 1939.
[12] Sara Evelyn Ward Thompson Eldert, personal papers.

ROBERT MOLFORD ADDISON

When his family first came to America, they lived for a short time in Providence, Rhode Island. When he was ten years of age, the family came West and settled in Iowa County, Wisconsin. He enrolled 13 August 1862 in Company E, 23 Regiment, Wisconsin Volunteers, as a private. From 13 August 1862 to 28 February 1863 he held the rank of corporal. They appointed him First Corporal on 1 April 1863, Sergeant on 13 April 1863 and First Lieutenant on 1 January 1864. When he enrolled at Mazomanie he was twenty-two years old, 5 feet 8 inches, fair complexion, brown hair and blue eyes. He was wounded slightly at the battle near Mansfield, Louisiana, on 8 April 1864. He saw action at Chickaway Bayou, Arkansas Post, Grand Gulf, Port Gibson, Champion Hills, Black River Bridge, Siege of Vicksburg, Jackson, Louisiana Forts Spanish and Blakely. He mustered out on 4 July 1865.

In 1895 James M. Bull, late Captain of Company E, 23rd Wisconsin, gave the following disposition: *Robert M. Addison was a brave and faithful soldier, cheerfully performing every known duty, and because of his worthiness deponent promoted him from private soldier, successively through all the grades of noncommissioned officer, and in due time recommended him for further promotion and obtained for him a commission as 2nd Lieutenant of said Co. "E." During the campaign against Vicksburg, Mississippi, in December 1862, in the Yazoo River Swamps and while in the line of his duty, Robert M. Addison contracted the disease, at the time known as "swamp fever" resulting in chronic diarrhea, indigestion, torpid liver, heart disease, piles, and rheumatism. All were intensified by the hardships and exposure of the Vicksburg campaign of 1863.* Captain Bull believed Robert Addison needed a furlough to save his life. He arranged the thirty day furlough after the surrender of Vicksburg, to visit his home at Black Earth, Wisconsin. He was home, sick, on renewed furlough for sixty days, and was then sent to the military hospital at Madison, Wisconsin, where he remained for some time. He returned to his company when possible, also bringing with him his commission as 1st Lieutenant, *but in a very feeble and emaciated condition.* At the battle of Sabine Cross Roads, Louisiana, 18 April 1864, while he was on staff duty, he was wounded in the face and neck. His physical disabilities originated in the "Yazoo Swamps." In November 1864, they promoted and transferred him to the 5th Wisconsin Volunteers.

Swamps." In November 1864, they promoted and transferred him to the 5th Wisconsin Volunteers.

After leaving the service, he lived first at Black Earth, Wisconsin; then about December 1865 moved to Quincy, Illinois; then about August 1867 to Owatonna, Minnesota; then about 1 August 1867 he went to Waseca, Minnesota and about 1 January 1873, he made his final move to Marshall, Minnesota. When he moved to Waseca, Minnesota, in 1867, he formed a partnership with William Everett, his brother-in-law. They built the first business building in that village and engaged in business there until they moved to Marshall late in 1872. They formed the firm of William Everett & Company, composed of William Everett, R. M. Addison and Charles A. DeGraff. DeGraff was in charge of the railroad contracting firm that was the putting the railroad through Lyon County. Mr. Addison hauled lumber from New Ulm and built the first business in the village. They were building the railroad, but they had not yet platted the town. They put up the frame shanty he built, 16X13 feet with a lean-to, directly in front of the site of the present Lyon County National Bank. The firm carried a large stock of goods and catered to railroad workers, who brought daily sales to $2000 to $2500. Mr. Addison also engaged in the tool business, in partnership with H. Tripp, who carried that mail between Redwood Falls and Lynd. The partners established their business in the corner behind the present Addison Block. In 1912 they conducted the business as R. M. Addison & Son. After the completion of the railroad to Marshall, Mr. Addison and S. H. Mott purchased the pioneer store of William Everett & Company. Two years later Addison became the sole proprietor of the business. He operated the store for a time in the building on the corner that Arthur Drew owned in 1912, and later occupied the Reichert Block. In 1887 he built the handsome business block he occupied, where he ran the hardware business exclusively. For a few years, Frank Reed was a partner in the business. About 1900 Harry Addison became his partner and the firm became "R. M. Addison & Son." He was living in Marshall, Minnesota in 1889, but he did not attend the reunions of the 23rd Wisconsin Regiment in 1886 or 1889.

He served as Mayor of Marshall and was Treasurer of Lyon County one term. He was a member of D.F. Markham Post No.7, Grand Army of the Republic. For more than twenty years, he was the vice-president of the First National Bank, an office he held at the time of his death. He suffered greatly the last year of his life, but they never knew him to complain, and passed away peacefully, surrounded by his family. They held the funeral services at his house, conducted by Bishop McElwain of the Episcopal church. Twenty members of the local order of the Grand Army of the Republic attended. The First National Bank, in honor of the departed vice-president, furnished a mammoth wheel of roses, with one broken spoke. *The death of no other citizen would cause greater sorrow among our people. Of an unassuming nature, he was, nevertheless, a man of action. His good deeds, while not heralded abroad, were many. His memory is cherished by scores of pioneer settlers befriended in financial and other ways in the days of long ago and by those whose friendship was obtained in later years and who honored and respected him for his sterling qualities* [13]

R.M. Addison
Marshall
Minn.

---

[13] Civil War Pension File, NARA, Robert M. Addison, application #1096678, certificate #1106045; Arthur P. Rose, *Illustrated History of Lyon County Minnesota* (Northern History Publishing Co; Marshall, MN, 1912), 280-281; Robert M. Addison obituary, *The News-Messenger*, Marshall, Minn. 16 Apr 1915 p1c1; Civil War Unit Histories, Part 4, The Union- Midwest and West: Regimental Histories and Personal Narratives. *The Survivors of the Twenty-third Regiment Wisconsin Volunteer Infantry*, 1889.

Twenty-third Infantry

Colonel- Joshua J. Guppey
Majors- Edmund Jussen, Charles H. Williams, William F. Vilas, Edgar P. Hill, Joseph E. Green
Lieutenant Colonels- Edmund Jussen, William F. Vilas, Edgar P. Hill

They organized the regiment at Camp Randall, Madison in August of 1862 and went to Cincinnati on September 15. They ordered it south to Vicksburg where it was in the assault on Chickasaw Bluffs and Arkansas Post. They went to Young's Point, Louisiana, near Vicksburg, where three-fourths of the men were stricken with a viral disease due to the lack of sanitary conditions. They were on scout and foraging assignments until 30 April 1863 when they brought them into reserve at Port Gibson. They entered the village the following day, being the first Union troops to occupy it. They engaged at Champion's Hill, and the following day went to Black River bridge where the brigade captured the 60th Tennessee. They reached Vicksburg on the 18th and participated in the general assault on the 22nd. They were on duty until the surrender, when they reduced their numbers to 150 men fit for duty. They were in the attack on Jackson, then joined the expedition to Barre's landing near Opelousas, which it occupied the entire summer. Their return march began November 1, and two days later a superior force attacked at Carrion Crow Bayou, driving two regiments through the 23rd's lines. The regiment, flanked on both sides, fell back. Reinforced, they drove the enemy back and regained the lost ground. They lost 128 out of the 220 engaged. They reached Brashear City on December 13 and were ordered to Texas, where they remained until 22 February 1864, when they returned to Louisiana. They participated in the Red River expedition, the battle of Sabine Cross-Roads, and the action at Cloutierville. They remained in camp at Baton Rouge from May 25 until July 8 then went to Algiers and Morganza where they remained until August 18. They transferred to the 3rd Brigade, 2nd Division, 19th Army Corps, engaging in guard, post, garrison and reconnaissance duty until 1 May 1865. They ordered them to Mobile, engaged in siege, patrol and picket duty and short expeditions until July 4, when it mustered out. Original strength 994; gained 123 by recruits; loss by death 289; missing one; desertion six; transferred 124; discharged 281; mustered out 416.[14]

---

[26] *The Union Army.* (Broadfoot Publishing Company, Wilmington, NC, 1998) IV: 59-60.

Battles

Sabine Cross Roads or Mansfield, Louisiana[15]

8 April 1864, Friday

The Confederates under General Richard Taylor formed a defensive line three miles southeast of Mansfield, after withdrawing 200 miles due to Bank's superior forces. It was there that Taylor decided to halt Bank's advance to Shreveport. The Federal expedition moved out on a road too far inland from the Red River. They strung them out in a long file, and had carelessly placed wagon trains in the line of march. Low water made the Union gunboats at Grand Encore useless to Banks, so he stopped and ordered his forces consolidated. Neither commander intended to fight a major engagement until the next day, but small units had already been engaged and at 4:00 P.M. Taylor struck in a disjointed attack. A full-scale shooting match resulted, known as Sabine Crossroads, Mansfield, or Pleasant Grove. Taylor estimates that he had 5,300 infantry, 3,000 cavalrymen and 500 artillerymen present. Banks' men were forced back and they lost several guns. They outflanked them on both sides and gave way with panic and confusion. A wagon train blocked the road of retreat, which added to the problems. At Pleasant Grove the troops of William H. Emory stood hard and the Southern attack died out. During the night Banks withdrew to Pleasant Hill and formed another defense line. One Yankee called it "our skedaddle from the rebs."

Federal casualties were high for an engaged force of about 12,000. 113 killed; 581 wounded; 1,541 missing; 2,235 captured. They also reported that they lost twenty guns and 250 wagons. Confederate losses are uncertain, but estimates are 1,000 killed and wounded out of approximately 8,800.

---

[15] Mark Mayo Boatner, *The Civil War Dictionary* (David McKay Company, Inc., New York) Revised Edition. P. 655, 715-716; F. B. Long, *The Civil War Day by Day An Almanac 1861-1865* (Doubleday & Company, Inc. (Garden City, NY, 1971. P. 482-483.

Pleasant Hill, Louisiana
9 April 1864, Saturday

General Banks' Federals expected another attack from the Confederates under General Taylor, and withdrew fifteen miles southeast to Pleasant Hill, Louisiana where General A. J. Smith's force had been left. General Richard Taylor pursued, and at first, the skirmishing was light. About 5:00 P.M. the Confederates made their main drive, gaining some ground and then pushing the Federals back to their reserve. A countercharge worked, and the Federals drove the Confederates back, ending the engagement as a Northern victory. The Federals withdrew to Grand Encore (near Natchitoches) the night of the battle, united with the rest of Bank's forces and entrenched. The Confederates left a cavalry screen and turned against Steele in Arkansas.

The Federals lost 1,369 out of 12, 247 (150 killed, 844 wounded, 375 missing). The Confederates lost about 1,500 out of 14,300 (1,200 killed and wounded; 426 missing).

- - - - - - - - -

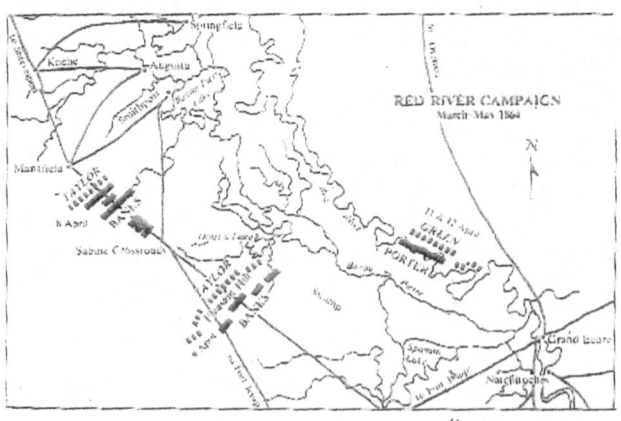

The Mississippi River Fleet

When the Southern states seceded, whoever controlled the Mississippi River would control the continent. The River was a principle north-south highway of commerce and communication, along with the network of other rivers that led to the Mississippi River. Control of the River would split the Confederacy, preventing the dispersal of food and supplies and reopening commerce for the Union Midwestern states.

In 1861, the United States Army got and built the first armored vessels. These first "timberclads" were the *Conestoga, Lexington,* and *Tyler*, were soon joined by better protected armored boats built by James B. Eads. Specially attached Navy officers commanded the Western Gunboat Flotilla steamers, although the Army operated them. After the failure of the first attack on Vicksburg, 1 October 1862, they transferred most of these Army vessels to the Navy as commissioned naval vessels.

Many flat-bottomed river steamers with their tall smoke pipes, both side-wheelers and stern-wheelers, were lightly armored. They bore identifying numbers on their pilothouses and were known as tin clads.

They named the Ellet rams, another group of ships, after their progenitor, Colonel Charles Ellet. He got several river boats and outfitted them as lightly armed rams, which he personally led into battle. They reinforced the hulls and bows with timber. They carried little or no armament. The Ellet rams formed an independent command that was never incorporated into the Navy, although it operated under Naval orders.

Larger heavily armored vessels appeared on the rivers, *Chactaw, Lafayette, Eastport.* They were powerfully armed ships with experimental armor that included useless rubber. During this period the Navy was building monitors designed specially for river operations. The *Ozark, Neosho,* and *Osage* and the four vessels of the *Milwaukee* class arrived in time to join in the fighting.

To wrestle control of the Mississippi River, the Federal forces attacked at both its northern and southern ends. The two-pronged drive hoped to meet midway and split the Confederacy. Farragut's deep-set Navy captured the major port of New Orleans in May 1862. In the North, supporting the Army, the makeshift armed river steamers left their base at Cairo, Illinois. They joined battle at Forts Henry and Donelson, Island No. 10 and Memphis, overcoming Confederate defenses.

Expeditions attempted to turn the enemy lines at Vicksburg up and around the Yazoo River, with success in April 1863. After almost a year of disappointments Vicksburg fell on 4 July 1863, giving the Union full control of the Mississippi along its entire length.

Union gunboats went up the Cumberland and Tennessee rivers through Kentucky and Tennessee and into Alabama. In 1864, the river fleet penetrated up the Red River in Louisiana and Arkansas, only to become trapped by the falling water level of the river. The heavy ironclads could escape down the river by the engineering of man-made dams and waterfalls.

The stern-wheel steamer *Cricket*, tinclad number 6, with other river steamers behind. (U.S. Naval Historical Center)

Civil War Diary

Thursday, December 24, 1863
Left Arena on my journey to join my Reg. Arrived at Madison on the 25th where I spent my Christmas.

Saturday, December 26, 1863
__ is on for today. I arrived at Chicago at 9 PM.

Monday, December 28, 1863
Left Chicago for Cairo. Arriving at Cairo on the 29th at 5 PM.

The troops met in and near Cairo, Illinois, where they moved to and from the front lines. The Wisconsin regiments left Camp Randall for Cairo via Chicago. Once in Chicago, the troops boarded trains of cattle's cars on the Illinois Central Railroad. The trip took two days to reach Cairo. It allowed for the stay over in Chicago, the number of times the train would stop for fuel or water, and the time for the soldier to stretch his legs from riding in the freight cars.[16]

Wednesday, December 30, 1863
Left Cairo for New Orleans on the steamer P. S. Swan.

Friday, January 1, 1864
Left Island No. 1.

---

[16] Regimental History- 42 Wisconsin Infantry- http://www.angelfire.com/sys/popup_source.shtml?Category; *Illinois Camps, Posts, and Prisons* by Victor Hicken, Illinois Civil War Sketches, No. 9, published by Illinois State Historical Library for the Civil War Centennial Commission of Illinois.

Extremely cold weather hit the North and South on this day, where temperatures dipped below zero in Cairo, Illinois, causing the soldiers much suffering.[17]

29th Wisconsin: This is the coldest day we have experience in the South. Ice formed in the wide, shallow, railway ditches near camp, a fourth of an inch in thickness. Many old residents of New Orleans came over the river to see it. Some old men who said they had always lived at New Orleans, said there had been ice from New York and Baltimore but that this was the first time they ever saw that grew here.[18]

Saturday, January 2, 1864

Continued steaming pleasantly down the river till 9 AM. We were then hailed by some military officers, ordering us up the steam a few miles to take on board at Lt. and four soldiers, who as been sent from Fort Pillow Dec 31st to arrest a steamer suspicioned as being a contraband trader. These four soldiers were overtaken by a severe storm last ___ and perished with cold. Arrived at Memphis at 9 PM.

The 1,250 acre Fort Pillow State Park is in Lauderdale County on the Chickasaw Bluffs, overlooking the Mississippi River. In 1861, the Confederate Army built extensive fortifications here and named the site for General Gideon J. Pillow of Maury County, a Mexican War hero. Because of its strategic location, the Union Army took the fort, who controlled it during most of the war. Today, remains of the earthworks are well-preserved. Early during the war, the Confederacy saw the necessity to defend it against a Union invasion by way of the Mississippi River. Fort Pillow was one of several fortifications constructed on the river as a part of a river defense system. They built the fort on Chickasaw Bluff No. 1 overlooking the river. Batteries of cannons were constructed facing the river. They dug an extensive system of

---

[17] E. B. Long, *The Civil War Day by Day AN ALMANAC 1861-1865* (Doubleday & Company, Inc.: Garden City, New York, 1971), 452.

[17] Civil War Unit Histories, Part 4, The Union- Midwest and West: Regimental Histories and Personal Narratives. *The Diary of a Private Soldier: the exact copy of a record kept day by day during the Civil War*, Henry P. Whipple of the 29th Wisconsin, p. 34.

breastworks for the protection of the river batteries in case of land attack. During the war the fort's river batteries were close to the

river, but since the war erosion factors have caused the river to move a mile west.[19]

Sunday, January 3, 1864

Left Memphis at __. Nothing of importance __ being a damp, disagreeable day . . . In the morning it snowed quite hard. There never was known to be so much snow in the City of Memphis for many years. Sailed __ this afternoon being __ and up on the __ side at dark.

Monday, January 4, 1864

Put on steam and left at day light. Arriving at Helena at 11 AM.

---

[18] Tennessee State Parks: Fort Pillow State Park-http://www.state.tn.us/environment/parks/pillow/

	Killed	Wounded	Missing
Fredericksburg	1,138	9,105	2,678
Chancellorsville	"	"	"
Gettysburg	2,834	13,709	6,640
Briston Station	51	329	
Fort Hudson	200	800	
Chickasaw Bayou 191	982	756	
Arkansas Post	129	831	
Port __	130	71_	
Mile __	4	34	
Raymond	69	241	_2
Jackson	40	240	
Champion Hills	426	1,842	189
Big Beach Railroad Bridge	29	242	2
Vicksburg	545	3,622	_08
Prairie Grove	161	793	185
Stone River	1,823		
—	1,644	924	
Bridgeport	76		22

Tuesday, January 5, 1864

Left Island No 65. Passed Napoleon at 11 AM.

Wednesday, January 6, 1864

Arrived at Goodricks Landing at daylight, where we stopped for wood. Stopped at Millikens Bend at 3 ½ PM. Arrived at Vicksburg at 6 PM. The city I found much cleaned and nicer looking than when I was there in Aug 1863. Quite a number of stores are in operation, but business is very dull compared with any of our northern city.

Thursday, January 7, 1864

All this morning was occupied in unloading the beef cattle brought south for the army. And unshipping the freight with which the boat was very heavily loaded. Most of the passengers stopped at Vicksburg. We left Vicksburg at 1 PM. Stopped by house for wood a few miles from Vicksburg. At 9 PM struck a snag in the bogs- sprung a leak. We were compelled to throw a great deal of freight overboard. We worked at the pumps all night.

Friday, January 8, 1864

4 PM still unable to move the boat. And being in a neighborhood infested with guerrillas and the Capt of the steamer dispatched a messenger down the river for the assistance of a gun boat. Two gun boats were immediately sent up from Rodney. And by lightening our load and working vigorously at the pumps we were enabled to get loose just before day. Sailed all night making excellent time. Passed Baton Rouge before daylight.

Saturday, January 9, 1864

We made most excellent time during the night. Passed Baton Rouge just before daylight. I think the scenery along the river from Baton Rouge to the Gulf is most beautiful. We stopped this afternoon at a most splendid plantation the planters private mansion was most magnificent. Arrived at New Orleans at 11 PM.

Sunday, January 10, 1864

Remained on the boat till this morning, I then went to the City and reported myself to the General and was transferred to the Convelescents Camp to wait till I procure transportation to my Reg which has gone to Texas.

Monday, January 11, 1864

I heard with great pleasure last night that my Col, Capt, and officers captured at Buzzards Prairie- were exchanged at the Charles Hotel I therefore went up this morning, and to my great pleasure met my Capt in the street opposite Charles. Out meeting was as happy as unexpected. And after congratulating me on my success we both had a good square dinner together.

Tuesday, January 12, 1864

This has been a cold rainy disagreeable day. Capt Donaldson commanding the camp put me on duty and am now acting as Officer of the day. I have inspected all the barracks. Had the Parade ground cleaned up and searched four men suspicioned for stealing a sum of money. I found the guilty one took the money and delivered the offender to the Post Commander.

Wednesday, January 13, 1864

This has been a cold disagreeable day. I have found employment in studying my tactics and Military regulations. This time last year I was at Arkansas Post. We had the battle on the 12th and on the 13th day- clearing the Fort of __.

Thursday, January 14, 1864

I spent the day in studying the tactics till 11 AM. I then had to go up to the city on business. In the afternoon I was pleased to meet 4 of the boys from my Co some of the same who were captured at Buzzards Prairie. They every one expressed their hardy satisfaction on hearing of my promotion.

Friday, January 15, 1864.

Spent the day prep Vols __ my boys who were captured at Buzzard's Prairie. We had a fine time talking over old times together and finished up the visit with several good games of chess.

Saturday, January 16, 1864

This has been a most beautiful day. The sun has shone with all his splendor, and we have had a __ bracing breeze making everyone feel cheerful. Spent the morning in company with __. This afternoon I have been looking around trying to get transportation to my Reg.

Sunday, January 17, 1864

Went up to the city in the morning with the intention of seeing my __. But I left so very __ I came back without seeing him.

Monday, January 18, 1864

I went down to the wharf and saw the Q. M. Capt Armstrong and procured transportation to my Reg.

Tuesday, January 19, 1864

Received orders from Maj Davidson to go on board the steamship Belvidier in charge of 140 men. Went on board at 9 PM.

Wednesday, January 20, 1864

Sailed all night, and arrived at the bar (mouth of the Miss river) at daylight Had a beautiful day the Gulf was very calm; consequently but a few were seasick.

Thursday, January 21, 1864

We have had another lovely day. The Gulf being quite calm we made rapid progress. Passed Galveston at 12 PM. And arrived near our destination at 10 PM.

Friday, January 22, 1864

We remained on board our vessel all day waiting for orders. We lay just in sight of the entrance of the bay and could just discern the distant camps of our div.

Saturday, January 23, 1864

I spent the night in assisting to unload the freight from our boat onto another of less draught of water. And the afternoon we crossed the bar.

Sunday, January 24, 1864

This has been a most lovely day. Not having a great deal to attend to I spent the day in walking around viewing our new camp in company with some of my old companions.

Monday, January 25, 1864

This has been a most splendid day, as the Reg just returned yesterday from a hard match and being tired we have not had drill. Consequently it has been an idle day in camp. I spent the afternoon in doing company writing. The evening I have devoted to my tactics.

Tuesday, January 26, 1864

Formed the Co at 9 AM and had company drill. Had Brigade drill in the afternoon from 2 o'clock till 4. Dress parade at 4 ½ .

Wednesday, January 27, 1864

This has been another most beautiful day. We have spent it in much the same manner as yesterday. Capt went to gather shells on the sea shore in the morning. So I drilled the company. Had battalion drill in the afternoon. And spent the evening in studying.

Thursday, January 28, 1864

I drilled the Co this morning in the bayonet exercise and had a very pleasant and interesting drill. In the afternoon the Reg was formed on the parade ground and we had a short drill in the material of arms. Our Reg drills beautifully. Our Brig has been strengthened by the addition of the 19th Ky Col Infy and the 77th Ill.

Friday, January 29, 1864

We have had a little rain today but nothing to interfere with drill. I drilled the Company in the bayonet exercise this morning. And we had Brig drilling the afternoon. As the Capt was brig officer of the day, I had to command the Co and managed much better than I expected. This is the first time I have commanded the Co on Brig drill.

Saturday, January 30, 1864

This has been another most lovely day. We had Company drill this morning. No battalion drill this afternoon many of the boys went fishing and I went to the sea shore and gathered some shells to send home.

Sunday, January 31 1864

Got up at daylight. Had Co inspection at 10 AM. Spent the rest of the day in reading an interesting book and in writing home. Took the Company on parade on 5 PM. Spent the evening reading and writing.

Monday, February, 1, 1864

This is another most splendid day. Exactly like another spring day in the north. I got up by daylight. Drilled the Co in the bayonet exercise in the morning. Had battalion drill at 2 PM. We received a mail tonight. Spent the evening in studying.

Tuesday, February 2, 1864

Had Battalion drill in the manual of arms, at 10 AM. And made a very good appearance. Had Brigade drill at 2 PM. We went through the different evolutions excellently. Our Div Commander Gen Ransin was present to see us drill. Dress parade at 5½ . And I devoted the evening to study.

Wednesday, February 3, 1864

Moved our position in the Reg from the extreme left to the extreme right. As the morning was pretty much taken up with moving, Co drill was dispensed with. Had review at 2 PM. Inspected by our Brigade Commander Col Laudram. Spent the evening company with Dr Wood, Maj Greene, Lt Atkinson and Capt Bull, Had a very pleasant visit together.

Thursday, February 4, 1864

Spent the day in the same old routine of camp life. Reveille just after day break. Took our frugel repast at 6 0'clock. Company drill at 11 AM. Had a very nice battalion drill at 2 PM. And spent the evening in study.

Friday, February 5, 1864

Had a good long company drill this morning in the bayonet exercise. At 2 PM marched out to our Brig drill ground where we had a very interesting Brigade drill. Dress parade at 5½. Issued the boys new clothing in the evening. Went to div Head Q on business. Spent the rest of the evening in answering my letters from home and studying the tactics.

Saturday, February 6, 1864

Our division was inspected and reviewed by Gen Ord at 9 AM. Made a very good appearance. The Gen complimented the 23 Wis highly. We had no drill this afternoon, so we went fishing. Co E and G had the use of the seive. Had good luck and caught quite a lot of fish.

Sunday, February 7, 1864

Had our regular Sunday morning inspection at 10 AM. I then had the remainder of the day at my own disposal, which I spent in various ways. Went down to the sea shore and had a good bathe. The Capt lent me very interesting book which I spent nearly all the rest of the day reading.

Monday, February 8, 1864

Drilled the Co in the skirmish drill at 10 AM. Met a friend from the 11th Wis for almost all the 11th have gone in as veterans. At 2 PM our Reg was drilled by Laudram the Brig Commander acquitted themselves finely. Dress parade at 5 ½ PM. At the conclusion of which an order was read issued by Gen Dana complimenting our Reg for their soldierly appearance on review on the 6 of Jan.

Tuesday, February 9, 1864

Skirmish drill at 10 Am. Rained in afternoon which prevented us from having Brigade drill. The Maj sent for all the company commanders. Wished them to send in a full resquestion for ordinance and camp equipage and turn all condemned property over to the Quarter Master. Spent a pleasant evening in playing checkers with Captains brother.

Wednesday, February 10, 1864

23rd had been on __ all day unloading __ and cord wood from the transport Corrinthaun. Received new clothing for the Co issued at night. Engaged in attending to some Company business this evening.

Thursday, February 11, 1864

Drilled the Co this morning on the bayonet exercise. I was pleased this morning on the arrival of 65 men formerly of the 11th Wis Vols. These are now assigned to our Reg. 10 have been put in our Co. Had no Batt drill this afternoon as the time was occupied in making arrangements for these new comers.

Friday, February 12, 1864

Company drill at 10 AM. Had a very interesting Brigade drill this afternoon Gen Ranson was on the ground watching four various movements. I must add that Gen Ranson is a gentle-man. I was in his company this evening and had some con-versation with him as a matter of business. He is something like Gen Grant, sociable and friendly with men of all ranks.

Saturday, February 13, 1864

Had a short squad drill this morning. No Battalion this afternoon and the boys have the privilege of going where they pleased. Some are starting to bathe in the bay, others are fishing and some have gone to gather shells.

Sunday, February 14, 1864

Detailed as Officer of the Day. Had quite a pleasant time during the day talking with the different officers and soldiers, as they came to the reserve to be passed through the lines. I was up all night, walking the picket line. Nothing of importance transpired during the night, and we were relieved at 10 next morning.

Monday, February 15, 1864

As soon as I arrived in Camp I found that the 11th Wis was then at the landing, just ready to start for home. I felt as if I must see the boys if it was forever. So short a time and so I hastened down, and made quite a visit before the boat started. Our Reg was inspected in the afternoon by Gen Ranson.

Tuesday, February 16, 1864

Had Co drill this morning in the manual of arms. Had a very interesting battalion drill in afternoon had two new movements forming oblong squares. And passing __ file by __ front. Just __ when the drums beat for dress parade. Spent the evening in studying the tactics.

Wednesday, February 17, 1864

Very cold and windy. Had Co drill this morning in the skirmish drill. As it was very cold it just suited the boys double quicking rallying by fours and sections assembling Co. No Brig drill on account of the weather. So I improved the opportunity of packing a box of shells to send home.

Thursday, February 18, 1864

Very cold, stormy and windy. The waves on the Gulf roll high. Tent blew down last night. Nothing to do tonight but study and read and try to keep warm by rolling up in plenty of good woolen blankets. Much rather be here in my sung little tent than tossing around on the Gulf of Mexico.

Friday, February 19, 1864

Still cold and windy. Had no Company drill this morning. But had a very interesting Brig drill this afternoon. Had a mail from the north. Recd a letter from Amelia.

Saturday, February 20, 1864

Been rather an idle day. Co drill at 10 AM. Maj Greene sent for all the Co Commanders had quite a debate on the propriety of furnishing the Reg with shelter tents. Most of the Co commanders were opposed to taking the tents. But it was finally settled that they should be issued. No Battalion drill this afternoon most of the Reg went fishing. I attended to some business of my own.

Sunday, February 21, 1864

Company E in fatigue. Reported at Brig Head Quarter at 8 AM. Crossed the Bay on the propeller Tyler for the purpose of unloading a steamer found another detail before us came back without working. Had a very pleasant boat ride on the bay.

Monday, February 22, 1864

Passed the day much as usual. About __ Maj Greene __ all the Co commanders. Informed us that we should move during the night, wished us to have our Camps in readiness with three days rations. Left our old camp at 11 PM and embarked in the steamship *Alliance*. Loaded all our tents, camp __. Remained at the landing till daylight.

They embarked on steamer *Alliance* February 22, sailed for Algiers, Louisiana that they reached February 26.[20]

Tuesday, February 23, 1864

Tuesday morning came bright and pleasant. Our gallant crew had on steam before daylight and away we went, out of the beautiful bay into the broad Gulf. Presently the wind raised and many of our boys became very seasick.

Wednesday, February 24, 1864

This has been a most delightful day. The Gulf has been almost as calm as a river. We have only our own Reg on board which made it much pleasanter.

Thursday, February 25, 1864

Still, proceed on our journey across the ___. This has been another calm lovely day. Passed Galveston about noon we were just near enough the Texas shore to enable us to catch a glimpse of the City. Entered the mouth of the river at day break came by the south east pas. Passed Fort Jackson at 2 PM and landed at Algiers at 2 next morning.

Friday, February 26, 1864

We unloaded our boat as rapidly as possible and reloaded our things again on the cars. And at 10 ___ started for Brasier City. I never passed through a more splendid country in my life. Had a delightful ride and arrived at Brasier at dark.

They took cars for Brashier City, Louisiana, arriving at 3:00 P.M. on the same day. They ferried them across Berwick Bay and camped at Berwick City.[21]

---

[19] Compiled Records Showing Service of Military Units in Volunteer Union Organizations- Company E, 23rd Wisconsin, NARA M594, roll 201.

[20] Compiled Records Showing Service of Military Units in Volunteer Union Organizations- Company E, 23rd Wisconsin, NARA M594, roll 201.

Saturday, February 27, 1864

We have been engaged straightening up our Camp. As we are located in a rough sugar field, we have had quite a task to level the ground. But we have our camp now in excellent order. And a pleasant camp it is. Situated on the banks of the Berwich Bay.

Sunday, February 28, 1864

Had inspection at 9 Am. Spent the rest of the morning in answering letters from home. Capt Bull returned from New Orleans arrived just at super time. I was highly pleased on the arrival of eight new recruits for our Company Wheeler and James Butler.

Monday, February 29, 1864

Quite a busy day as it is the last day of the month the muster rolls had to made out the Company inspected and mustered. Received orders to be ready to march tomorrow.

Tuesday, March 1, 1864

March comes in very cold and stormy. It commenced raining in the night and has been very cold all day. I have been working at the muster rolls and descriptive rolls all day. Our tents were not turned over as was ordered last night for the good reason that it has been so very unpleasant.

Wednesday, March 2, 1864

Still cold and chilly. But much pleasanter than yesterday. Spent the morning in working at the muster rolls. I had Segt Roberts drill the Company this morning. Company drill again at 2 PM. As we had finished the rolls I took the Company out. Spent the evening in posting of the clothing and descriptive books.

Thursday, March 3, 1864

This has been a beautiful day. Had Company drill at 10 AM. Also at 2 PM. Dress parade at 5½. Spent the evening in studying the tactics.

Friday, March 4, 1864

This has been a very pleasant day. Nothing of importance occurred. Co drill at 10 Am. And at 2 PM drilled the skirmish drill.

Saturday, March 5, 1864

The same routine of camp life. Company drill in the morning. It being Saturday Maj Greene __ the drill.

Sunday, March 6, 1864

Regimental inspection at 9 AM. K's orders from Div Head Qts all our wedge tents were turned over and all prepared for marching tomorrow.

Monday, March 7, 1864

Struck our tents at 6 AM and started __. It has been quite a pleasant day to march. After marching about 15 miles we camped for the night on a __ grassy __ of ground __ to Bayau __.

They left camp at Berwick City, Louisiana and camped three miles beyond Franklin, Louisiana.[22]

Tuesday, March 8, 1864

Reveille at 4 AM breakfast at 4 ½. Started at 6. Marched off very briskly. Arrived at Franklin at 1 halted a short distance from the __ for dinner. Proceeded our march, pitched our tents at 5 ½ close to the Rayin __.

---

[21] Compiled Records Showing Service of Military Units in Volunteer Union Organizations- Company E, 23rd Wisconsin, NARA M594, roll 201.

Wednesday, March 9, 1864

Rainy, disagreeable today. I was detailed to take charge of a foraging party. Went out in the country to an old planter who had taken the oath of allegiance. We had loaded six wagons the owner refused to take the __ a receipt. So the Gen ordered us to unload the corn. We then were obliged to go in the field and husk what we took.

Thursday, March 10, 1864

Received a letter from Amelia. No drill today. I spent the day in visiting and attended to some Co business. Nine or ten of my boys went foraging and had good luck. It was amusing to see them come in laden with chickens, pigs and beef.

Friday, March 11, 1864

This has been a beautiful day. As we had two days run our Maj thought a little drill would not hurt us. Consequently we had skirmish drill in the morning at 10 AM. Also at 2 PM. Then I spent an hour in drilling the recruits. And at 5 ½ had dress parade.

Saturday, March 12, 1864

Co drilled at 9 AM. In the afternoon we __ the guns for the recruits also clothing. Some of our tents were turned over and we now tent by Div. We put our fly moved out table and took Capt Tolford as an inmate. Recd of T. H. Bull 4 __ Enfield rifles complete 4 sets of accoutrements. Segt Roberts __ Shaddruck left Co on account of sickness. Turned over their arms and accountrements complete to Pri Butler and Porter.

Sunday, March 13, 1864

Dispensed with the usual Sunday morning inspection. Regimental inspection at 3 PM. Made out inventories and receipts in triplicate of Ordinance stores, clothing and garrison equipage.

Monday, March 14, 1864

Sent our pay rolls to New Orleans. Received and issued clothing. Six dress coats and eight pr shoes, four pr socks and rubber blankets.

Tuesday, March 15, 1864

Company drill in the morning at 10. I sent Segt Roche to drill the Co. I drilled the recruits and Recd orders to march at 6 AM tomorrow.

Wednesday, March 16, 1864

Reveille at 4 struck our tents at daylight. And at daylight we commenced our march. We marched fast until 12 ½ O'clock. We then encamped for the night by the side of the Tachhe. The day being cool it made it pleasant marching. There was no straggling.

They left camp near Franklin, Louisiana and arrived at Alexandria, Louisiana on March 26, having marched about 150 miles.[23]

Thursday, March 17, 1864

Broke up our camp at __ AM and took the lead of the 1st Brig. Passed through New __ at noon. We marched through a most splendid country and went into camp at __ PM at Camp Pratt. Then the boys made a break for the beef cattle on the Prairie and soon returned loaded with fresh meat.

Friday, March 18, 1864

Reveilled at 4 and commenced our march at 6. Our route today was through a most splendid Prairie county inhabited almost entirely by the french. Arrived at Vernillian Bazin at 3 PM. Our Reg encamped on __ the other side. I was detailed to assist the train in passing over the pontoon bridge.

---

[22] Compiled Records Showing Service of Military Units in Volunteer Union Organizations- Company E, 23rd Wisconsin, NARA M594, roll 201.

Saturday, March 19, 1864

Broke up our camp at Vermillian Ba__ and commenced our march at 7 AM. Marched about 20 miles and encamped on the old battle ground of Carrian Craw Bayou.

Sunday, March 20, 1864

Reveille at 4 ½. Commenced our march at 6 o'clock. Passed through Copelousas at noon. Here our boys met many families that they had met on the battle ground of Carrin Crow. Passed through Washington at two. The 19th AC was encamped just west of the town on the Atchfalyaya River.

Monday, March 21, 1864

Purchased at Post Commissary, 3 P. coffee $1.75, 3 ½ candles .83. Rested at out camp on the Atchafalaya today. And the 19th Corps advanced. It has been a rainy, disagreeable day. Except to march again early in the morning.

Tuesday, March 22, 1864

Reveille at 5 Oclock. Commenced our march at 7 AM. Our Reg led this in and my Col G were the advanced guard. We made good time up withstanding the muddy condition of the roads. We marched 17 miles and went into camp on an old rebs plantation. On the way the boys made the poultry and pigs suffer was by no means slow.

Wednesday, March 23, 1864

Broke up our camp at 4 AM. And our column was in motion at 5. Our Reg was Rear Guard. Marched 21 miles encamped at __ Oclock.

Thursday, March 24, 1864

Continued our march. 77 Ill taking the advance of our column. 19 Ky next, ours next. Rained very hard, roads very muddy.

Friday, March 25, 1864

Broke up our camp and continued our march at 7 AM. Marched 15 miles. Went into camp at 3 PM. 5 miles south of Alexandria.

Saturday, March 26, 1864

Broke up our camp at 7 AM. Marched through Alexandria at noon. Went into camp 4 miles north-west of the town. Maj Greene informed us that we should rec 2 months pay. Sat up till midnight and made out the pay rolls.

Sunday, March 27, 1864

Maj Bridgen arrived to pay off our Reg. Refused to pay any who were not present at the muster the 21 of Dec. All the officers dissatisfied. The Pay master agrees to pay us for four months if we will wait two weeks. We accept the proposition.

Monday, March 28, 1864

Reville at 4½. Marched at 6. It rained very hard and the roads were very muddy the first __ of the day. Our Co and I were Rear guard of our __ train. Marched 16 miles went into camp at 4 PM.

They left camp near Alexandria and arrived at Natchitoches, Louisiana on April 2, a distance of about ninety miles.[24]

Tuesday, March 29, 1864

We remained in camp till noon as we were ordered to await the arrival of the ammunication train and guard and assist it through. We marched all day through a thick pine forest. Camped at dark on a cotton plantation. Found the old lady of the house very kind. She cooked us chicken eggs.

---

[23] Compiled Records Showing Service of Military Units in Volunteer Union Organizations- Company E, 23rd Wisconsin, NARA M594, roll 201.

Wednesday, March 30, 1864

Continued our march with the train through the pine woods. Arrived at 2 PM at Cane River. Here we found the rest of our Brig encamped and we soon pitched out tents for the night.

Thursday, March 31, 1864

Reveille at 4 AM. Commenced our march at 6 AM. Very dusty and disagreeable marching. Marched 19 miles and encamped on the side of the Cane River.

Friday, April 1, 1864

Reveille at 6. Commenced our march at 8 AM. All along the road could be seen the property destroyed by the rebel. They burnt almost all the cotton and forge on the road to prevent it from falling into our hands. Marched 16 miles and went into camp at 3½ PM.

Saturday, April 2, 1864

Our company and I were Rear Guard again. Arrived at our camp 4 miles south of Natchitoches at __ pitched out tents. Soon orders came for our Reg to pull up stake and move up to town, which we did and are now stationed here as patrol guards.

Sunday, April 3, 1864

I was detailed this day as Officer of the Patrol. Had charge of 60 men and 6 non-commissioned officers. My instructions were to arrest every soldier who had not a pass approved by their Div commanders. I also stationed guards at several houses. Everything went off quite smoothly for a Secesh Town. [secessionist town]

The Thirteenth Corps set out for Natchitoches, eighty miles away, on the 28th, reaching there on April 2. They assigned them to provost duty: Major Green commanding the post, Adjutant Carl Jussen acting as Post Adjutant, Captain Duncan was Provost Marshall, and Lieutenant Atkinson as Assistant Provost Marshal. [25]

Monday, April 4, 1864

I was relieved this morning by L. Stanley. The citizens houses were searched today, found many firearms. Recd a mail this afternoon, read three letters from home.

Tuesday, April 5, 1864

This has been a very pleasant day indeed, so pleasant that it was hard to sit writing all day in my tent. But business before pleasure. And after close application for nearly all day I at last completed the tedious task of making out my Quarterly Ordinance returns for the 1st quarter of 1864.

Wednesday, April 6, 1864

Broke our camp at Natchitoches and joined our Div at 6 AM. Marched 16 miles and camped.

---

[24] E. B. Quiner, Esq., *The Military History of Wisconsin* (Chicago: Clarks & Co. Publishers, 1866), 716.

Brig. General Thomas E. G. Ransom's detachment moved from Natchitoches at 6:00 A.M., in front of the infantry column and in the rear of the calvary division. The baggage trains of the calvary constantly delayed them. They overtook the calvary train and Dudley's brigade of the calvary and the head of the column arrived at Pleasant Hill at 2:00 p.m. They marched sixteen miles on the Pleasant Hill road and went into camp late on Bayou Mayon.[26]

Thursday, April 7, 1864

Reveille at 4 ½ Oclock. Marched at 6. Very hot and scarce of water. Our advanced cavalry drove the enemy but lost 80 men in killed and wounded. Marched about 19 miles and went into camp at Pleasant Hills.

They moved at 5:30 a.m. the head of the column arriving at Pleasant Hill, 19 miles, at 2:00 p.m., overtaking the cavalry train on the road and Dudley's brigade of cavalry at Pleasant Hill. Once the calvary had moved from their camping-ground, they were able to get into camp about 4:00 p.m. The train and rear guard did not arrive until late at night.

[The last of the infantry and all of the wagons were slowed due to the heavy storm that broke over the rear of the column and cut up the road very badly.][27] At 10:00 p.m., Ransom received an order to send a brigade of infantry to General Lee, and to be with him by daylight the next morning. At or before 5:00 a.m. Ransom directed Colonel Landram to move at 3:00 a.m. with the First Brigade of his division, and report to General Lee, 8 miles in front, at daylight or as soon after that as practicable.[28]

---

[24] *The War of the Rebellion: A Compilation of the Official Records of the Union and Confederate Armies* (Washington: Government Printing Office. 1893), Series I-Volume XXXIV, Part 1- Reports, No. 8, Red River Campaign, Brig. General T. E. G. Ransom, 264-268.

[25] Richard B. Irwin, History of the Nineteenth Army Corps (G. P. Putnam's Sons: New York, 1892), 297.

[25] *The War of the Rebellion: A Compilation of the Official Records of the Union and Confederate Armies* (Washington: Government Printing Office. 1893), Series I-Volume XXXIV, Part 1- Reports No. 8, Red River Campaign, Brig. General T. E. G. Ransom, 264-268.

Friday, April 8, 1864

Broke up our camp at 2 AM and marched to the front met the enemy at daylight. Skirmished all the morning driving the enemy before us. Marched 10 miles and met the enemy in force. The enemy hurled their whole force of about 20,000 against our little Brig and as we had no support they drive us capturing many prisoners and a great deal of our train.

Pleasant Hill, Louisiana- Colonel Landram moved with the First Brigade of his division and reported to General Lee at daylight. Under orders from Major-General Franklin, Ransom moved the remainder of the corps forward at 5:30 a.m., and arrived with the advance at Saint Patrick's Bayou, 10 miles, at 10:30 a.m., the march having, as before, been retarded by the cavalry train. General Franklin had previously designated a creek as their camping-ground, and Ransom accordingly ordered the Third Division and the Second Brigade of the Fourth Division into camp at 10:45 a.m. Before they had carried out the order, they received a request from General Lee for more infantry to relieve that already with him, and General Franklin directed Ransom to send forward the Second Brigade, Fourth Division, Col. J. W. Vance commanding, to relieve the First Brigade, whom they reported as worn out with hard skirmishing and marching. The Second Brigade moved forward at 11:00 a.m., and, at his request, General Franklin ordered Ransom to the front, to see that they relieved the First Brigade by the Second. Ransom immediately went forward, and at noon, on the road received a dispatch from Colonel W. J. Landram stating "My men have skirmished and marched through the bushes and thickets for eight or nine miles, making in all a march of 15 or 16 miles. They have no water, and are literally worn out. Can you have them relieved soon? General Lee insists on pushing ahead." [Landram, "The timber on each side of the road was heavy and dense, which rendered it very difficult to move in line, and the marching was tedious and tiresome to the men, the enemy contesting every foot of the ground as we advanced. All the houses near the road were abandoned, and we saw frequent evidence of large camps which had been recently deserted.] **The infantry finding much difficulty in passing the cavalry train, which obstructed the road, Ransom went on in advance of them, and arrived at the front, five and a half miles from Saint Patrick's Bayou, about 1:30 p.m.**

[Bank's force was stretched out the length of a long day's march on a single narrow road in a dense pine forest, with no elbowroom save such as was to be found in the narrow and infrequent clearings. In such a region excess of numbers was a hindrance rather than a help, and cavalry were worse than useless for offence. Banks was encumbered by twelve miles of wagons being all of his ammunition and stores. It was also weakened by the necessity of guiding the long train through the barren wilderness deep in the heart of the enemy's country.]²⁹ **He found that their forces had just driven the enemy across an open field, and were shelling him from a fine position on a ridge, which Colonel Landram occupied with his infantry and Nims' battery about 2:00 p.m. It was determined to halt here to allow the Second Brigade to come up and relieve the First. In company with Brigadier-General Stone and Lieutenant Higbie, signal officer, he went to the front of the line of skirmishers and carefully reconnoitered the position of the enemy. They could perceive two batteries and a large force of infantry in line of battle in the edge of the woods, from one-half to three-fourths of a mile to their front, and also considerable bodies of infantry moving down the road leading to their right and rear. Hearing of the arrival of Major-General Banks and staff upon the field, about 3:00 p.m. Ransom reported to him and advised him of the position and apparent strength of the enemy, and from him received instructions as to the disposition of his troops then on the field and of those momentarily expected. Upon the arrival of the Second Brigade, Major Lieber assigned the positions of two of its regiments, the Eighty-third and Ninety-sixth Ohio Infantry, on the opposite flank. The infantry on the right of the road occupied a narrow belt of timber dividing two large plantations. There was open ground in front and in back of the cultivated fields, which descended to a small creek. It then arose to the edge of the timber, one-half mile to the rear of their line.**

---

²⁷ Richard B. Irwin, *History of the Nineteenth Army Corps* (G. P. Putnam's Sons: New York, 1892), 300-301.

[Landram- "At a point about four miles from Mansfield, our advance came in sight of a wide opening in the timber in front of a hill of considerable height, on the right, left, and top of which there was considerable timber, but not so thickly set as on the road over which we had advanced. I had made frequent requests, before coming to this point, to have the brigade relieved or allowed to rest, inasmuch as the men were excessively fatigued by the loss of sleep and the difficulty experienced in advancing through the underbrush, which seemed to extend for miles to the right and left of the road, and was by General Lee that he had sent for the Second Brigade of my division to relieve the First."] **Nims' battery was posted on a hill near the road about 200 yards to the left of the belt of timber, and was supported by the Twenty-third Wisconsin Infantry, which was on the left and behind the crest of the hill with open fields in the front.** [The clearing was the largest yet seen by the Union Army since entering the wilderness of pines, was barely half a mile in width and across the road it stretched for about three quarters of a miles and down the middle it was divided by a ravine.][30] **The Sixty-seventh Indiana supported the battery on the right, joined by the Seventy-seventh Illinois, One hundred and thirtieth Illinois, Forty-eighth Ohio, Nineteenth Kentucky, Ninety-sixth Ohio, a section of mounted artillery, and the Eighty-third Ohio, making in all 2,413 infantries. The cavalry and mounted infantry, under General Lee, were posted on the flanks and rear, having Colonel Dudley's brigade on the left and Colonel Lucas' on the right, and skirmishers deployed in front of the infantry. The skirmishing continued throughout the afternoon, becoming sharp on the right about 2:30 p.m. At this time Colonel Lucas reported that they drove his skirmishers on the extreme right in, and that they captured a few of his men on that flank.** [2:30 p.m.- The 161st New York- "A courier is coming down the road at a rapid pace and rides directly to Headquarters flags and hands over his dispatch, a glance at them and the staff immediately mounts and leaves on a gallop. We are putting two days rations of hard tack in our haversacks, 2:50 p.m. bugle sounds, men fall in, 3:01 we file into the road and start at a lively pace, we are marching light, not even a blanket, everything left with the guard. We are stripped for a fight, cartridge boxes filled and twenty extra rounds in our pockets. It is

---

[28] Richard B. Irwin, *History of the Nineteenth Army Corps* (G. P. Putnam's Sons: New York, 1892), 302.

fearfully hot. After an hour's march we slow a little, but no halt; we are "marching to the sounds of the guns" which they can now plainly hear; 5:40 aide comes in from the front, with orders to make haste, the order rings out sharp and quick, "right should shift, forward double quick, march," and we start into a dog trot, it is a heart breaking pace, but the men are equal to it. An ambulance carrying General Ransom has just passed us; he is badly wounded.] **29th Wisconsin- "At the first rebel volley upon our right flank, Ransom was shot through both legs.** [A bullet knocked Ransom from his horse with a severe wound to his left knee. From the ground he shouted orders, trying to form up his troops until two strong infantrymen picked him up and carried him from the field.]^{31} **Colonel Hancock of the 29th set him against a tree. The men were falling fast on all sides. The general said to Hancock, "They are enfilading us. Tell the men to save themselves the best way they can. Leave me here; they will not hurt me." However, they put in an ambulance and took him from the field."]**
^{32} [We are now meeting the usual number of camp followers and Negroes, some mounted, a swearing, yelling mob, who shout "go back, you can't get through, we are whipped." Two or three companies are thrown out in effort to stop the rout, but it has not the slightest effect. We soon meet the masses of fleeing cavalry and the men of the 13th corps. How they shout and cheer, "19th boys, bully boys," and when some of the boys ask them what is the trouble they would shout back, "Hell, whipped, whipped by piece meal. Dick Taylor's whole army is just beyond the woods." It was every man for himself and the devils take the hindmost. I heard Gen. Franklin say the retreat was worse than Bull Run. It is utterly impossible to stay them, and the order is given to file to the right and get through the woods as quick as possible in any way we can. We finally filtered (filtered is just the word for it) through the woods and as we broke through and came into the open the men came together as one man and formed without a halt and filed into the Mansfield road on a run. As the regiment debouched into clearing, Dudley raised in his stirrups, waving his saber high in the air with dramatic gesture he shouted "halt, men, halt, here comes the 161st. By

---

^{29} William Riley Brookshire. *War Along the Bayous. The 1864 Red River Campaign in Louisiana* (Brassey's, 1998), 99.
^{26} Civil War Unit Histories, Part 4, The Union- Midwest and West: Regimental Histories and Personal Narratives. *The Diary of a Private Soldier: the exact copy of a record kept day by day during the Civil War*, Henry P. Whipple of the 29th Wisconsin, 79.

God you'll never see them run." We found it just as the 13th boys said, Dick Taylor's whole army was in the woods on the other side of the clearing.] [33] **About 4:00 p.m. the enemy commenced advancing his lines across the open fields in our front and east of the road. He directed Colonel Landram to advance our right, consisting of the Eighty-third, Ninety-sixth, and Forty-eight Ohio, One hundred and thirtieth Illinois, and Nineteenth Kentucky, and he immediately opened fire on the enemy, now in good range and advancing in two lines.** [Landram- "prisoners stated the enemy numbered 8,000 infantries, with a reserve of 12,000 cavalry and infantry. His entire force numbered 2,413 men."] **They drove back his first line in confusion upon his second, but recovering he again advanced till, unable to endure our heavy fire, he halted about 200 yards from their front, where many of his men laid down and returned our fire. He felt confident that this portion of their line could not be broken, but while moving toward the left flank they informed him that the enemy was pressing their left and that the mounted infantry there was falling back. At this time Captain White, chief of artillery, reported that the Chicago Mercantile Battery, Lieutenant Cone commanding, had arrived, and he directed Ransom to place them in an advantageous position on a ridge to the east of the road and near a house occupied as General Bank's headquarters, when they opened on the enemy, who had shown himself in strong force on the left. He sent Lieut. G. I. Davis, aide-de-camp, to order Lieutenant-Colonel Baldwin, commanding Eighty-third Ohio, to move his regiment to the support of the Twenty-third Wisconsin. He moved promptly, but they already drove the Twenty-third Wisconsin and the mounted infantry back, and he directed him to support the batteries. They now completely turned their left flank, and the enemy, having taken Nim's battery, were in strong force on the hill and pouring a destructive fire into the batteries of the Fourth Division. He ordered the latter to the rear to a point on the right of the road and sent Captain Dickey, his assistant adjutant-general, to order Colonel Landram to withdraw his division to the edge of the timber in our rear. Captain Dickey was to send aides to the different regiments to give them the orders direct in case he should**

---

[25] Civil War Unit Histories, Part 3, The Union- Mid-Atlantic, Roster and Monograph 161st Reg't, N.Y.S. Volunteer Infantry by J. W. Merwin, 121-122.

not find Colonel Landram, but while in the performance of this duty this gallant officer fell senseless from his horse, mortally wounded. Due to the loss of Captain Dickey before he had expressed Ransom's orders, some regiments did not receive them till they surrounded them and cut their retreat while they were gallantly fighting a superior force in front. Colonel Landram was reforming the line in the edge of the woods, when he was severely wounded in the knee and carried to the rear. He found the woods and roads filled with mounted men, flying in confusion from the field. [29th Wisconsin- "Just after crossing Cane River on the retreat down Red River from Sabine Cross-Roads. Our calvary had with them four pieces of mountain howitzers, which they used as flying artillery. There were four horses to each gun and a rider on each horse; the balance of the battery men was riding the gun carriages and caissons; the horses were going at a sharp gallop trying to get the range of the retreating rebels; the riders would turn their horses to bring the guns pointing to the front, halt a second to fire, and away they would go, every man in his place, the gunners loading the guns and the horses running, and then another gun would come up and go through the same performance. They kept it up for some miles, until there was not a rebel in sight."][34] Ransom praised the gallantry of Brigadier-General Stone, who was on the left of the line with General Lee. He used the small force of infantry to the best advantage in bravely but unsuccessfully trying to repulse the overwhelming force of the enemy. Colonel Landram, commanding Fourth Division, was conspicuous and everywhere present encouraging all by his own gallant conduct and judicious dispositions of his men. Colonel Vance, Ninety-sixth Ohio Infantry ably seconded his efforts, commanding Second Brigade, whom they killed, and by Colonel Emerson, of the Sixty-seventy Indiana Infantry, commanding First Brigade, whom they wounded and taken a prisoner. He was an eye witness of the bravery and soldierly bearing of Lieutenant-Colonel Cowan and Major Mann, of the Nineteenth Kentucky, Lieutenant-Colonel Baldwin, Eighty-third Ohio, Major Bering, Forty-eighth Ohio, Major Reid, One hundred and thirtieth Illinois, and knows

---

[28] Civil War Unit Histories, Part 4, The Union- Midwest and West: Regimental Histories and Personal Narratives. *The Diary of a Private Soldier: the exact copy of a record kept day by day during the Civil War*, Henry P. Whipple of the 29th Wisconsin, p. 80.

the gallantry with which their men repulsed the enemy in his first attack. The Twenty-third Wisconsin, Major Greene commanding, Sixty-seventh Indiana, Major Sears commanding, and the Seventy-seventh Illinois, Major Burdett commanding, are reported to him by Generals Stone and Lee to have acted nobly, meeting steadily the assaults of a very superior force of the enemy. He thanked the officers of his staff, Dr. J. S. McGrew, surgeon-in-chief, Captain Buel, aide-de-camp, Capt. P. H. White, chief of artillery, Lieutenant Tredway, aide-de-camp, Capt. P. H. White, chief of artillery, Lieutenant Richardson, acting inspector-general, and Lieutenant-Colonel Hatch, assistant quartermaster, all of whom performed their whole duty and rendered him valuable assistance. Lieutenants Higbie and Harris, signal officers, Captain Vilas and Lieutenants Ayers and Landram, of Colonel Landram's staff, were also distinguished for praiseworthy conduct. The Chicago Mercantile Battery, Lieutenant Cone commanding and the First Indiana Battery, Captain Klauss commanding, went promptly into action and behaved with gallantry. When the second line was broken, they would have brought off their guns in safety had it not been that out line of retreat was blocked up by the train of the cavalry. Captain White, chief of artillery, was in this battle, as in all others, distinguished for coolness and excellent judgment. He was captured with Lieutenant Cone while attempting to save the battery. Ransom felt it was his duty to record the disgraceful conduct of Lieutenant-Colonel Lindsey, of the Forty-eighth Ohio Infantry, whom he saw at some distance in the rear of his regiment lying behind a fallen tree, while his veteran regiment was in the thickest of the fight under the lamented Major Bering. They repulsed a superior force in their front, and but for the movement of a large body of the enemy upon their left flank, which the force at their command could not prevent, would have held the first line, and with the assistance of General Cameron's (Third) division could have checked the enemy till the arrival of the Nineteenth Corps. Soon after Ransom was wounded, General Cameron arrived with the Third Division, and took command of the detachment of the Thirteenth Army Corps.[35]

---

[26] *The War of the Rebellion: A Compilation of the Official Records of the Union and Confederate Armies* (Washington: Government Printing Office, 1893), Series I-Volume XXXIV, Part 1- Reports, No. 8, Red River Campaign, Report of Brig. General

Saturday, April 9, 1864

Were retreating all night arrived at Pleasant Hills this morning at 6 AM. Found Gen. A. J. Smith waiting with his army to give them a turn. Our Div continued to move right and Smith fought them in the after noon whipping them badly, capturing about 2,000 prisoners and literally strewing the ground with the rebel dead.

8:00 a.m. the 161st NY arrived in Pleasant Hills, "tired and ugly, but plenty of fight in the men yet, in fact, fight is what the men wanted just now. Men will talk, and they talk very plain at times, and this is one of the times, but they feel that the old first division can whip anything going if they are given half a chance. We are resting as well as possible now, the rebels are all around us, and we look for a fight some time before night. Pleasant Hill is a small hamlet, not over 15 or 20 dwellings, and is on the main road from Natchitoches to Shreveport." [36]

They retreated toward Grand Encore, Louisiana, which they reached on April 11.[37]

Sunday, April 10, 1864

Marched all last nite and all today. Camped at night about 15 miles from the river.

Monday, April 11, 1864

Our Reg was ordered to guard the prisoners through. Arrived at the river at 3 PM.

Thomas E. G. Ransom, 264-268; Series I-Volume XXXIV, Part 1- Reports p.290-294 No. 20, Red River Campaign, Report of Colonel William J. Landram.

[28] Civil War Unit Histories, Part 3, *The Union- Mid-Atlantic, Roster and Monograph 161st Reg't, N.Y.S. Volunteer Infantry* by J. W. Merwin, 121-122.

[27] Compiled Records Showing Service of Military Units in Volunteer Union Organizations- Company E, 23rd Wisconsin, NARA M594, roll 201.

They reached Grand Encore on the eleventh and were occupied in guarding prisoners there, until they affected an exchange on the nineteenth.[38]

Tuesday, April 12, 1864

Remained in camp at the Red River. Been employed today in writing and doing business.

Wednesday, April 13, 1864

On duty today as officer of the guard. My business was to guard the prisoners that we had captured. At 1 PM our Reg was ordered to the front and I joined my Co. Marched to the front and took a position in the dense woods, our boys then commenced cutting down the timber making it almost impossible for the rebels to charge on our line.

Thursday, April 14, 1864

Our line was surveyed by the engineers. A change of position was decided upon and we moved. Spent the day in building fortifications.

---

[37] E. B. Quiner, Esq., *The Military History of Wisconsin* (Chicago: Clarks & Co. Publishers, 1866), 717.

The tired and disgruntled troops were ordered to begin fortifying the village. While they all were not eager for that type of duty, some took comfort knowing they would be protected. A member of the 83rd Ohio noted, "A retreating army is very sensitive to the sound of firearms, reports of danger, etc." They laid out a line of breastworks of logs and earth around the village, then it was covered with a thick layer of packed dirt. In front of the fortifications, they cut down all the trees. Most of the troops worked on the fortifications, while others went into the countryside, foraging. This duty was very dangerous, as the woods were infested with not only Confederate troops but guerrillas that held no allegiance to either side. The insects were intolerable and a member of the 114th New York complained about the wood ticks and worried about scorpions.[39]

Friday, April 15, 1864

Remained in the same place. Nothing of importance occured.

Saturday, April 16, 1864

Still in the same position. Moved our camp equipage up from the rear. And we now have out tents and are encamped behind our fortifications. Eight Oclock PM it is now rumored that we shall leave here in the morning.

Sunday, April 17, 1864

All is quite in our Brig. Had Co inspection at 9 AM. There as been a detail working all day strengthening our fortifications. This is rather an indication of remaining for the present.

Monday, April 18, 1864

Inspection at 10 AM in heavy marching order. Spent the afternoon in attending to Co business making out monthly returns.

---

[36] William Riley Brooksher. *War Along the Bayous. The 1864 Red River Campaign in Louisiana.* Brassey's, 1998.p.161-163.

Tuesday, April 19, 1864

This has been a fine pleasant day, nothing of importance occured. Jacob Wikoff arrived at 9 PM with a mail for Brig. Recd three good cheering letters from home. Rec orders to be ready to move at an hours notice.

Wednesday, April 20, 1864

Still remain at Grand Encore. The sick were sent down the river today. Gilbert Harris was sent back from my Co Ben Parkin detailed in __ Corps. Just rec orders to be ready to march at 5 PM.

They put the sick and wounded on transports to be sent down river and correspondent J. E. Hayes of the *New York Tribune* wrote about the callous manner in which they treated the sick and wounded.[40]

Thursday, April 21, 1864

Commenced our march towards Alexandria. Marched about 4 miles came to a halt, lay at our arms all night and we discovered by the different maneuvers of the cavalry and the columns of Infy that continued to __ that a general retreat had been ordered. The 19th Corps passed at 2 AM and we followed directly after them.

Friday, April 22, 1864

Continued our march, arrived at Cane River at day light, which we crossed at day light. This retreating is most miserable business, something that the 13 ac never has been used to before. But as it was impossible to procure supplies and they also greatly out numbered us, we were obliged to fall back to the river. The rebs were close in our rear. Marched all day and till 2 next morning. When we halted for about 2 hours to rest, just east of Cloutierville.

---

[37] William Riley Brooksher. *War Along the Bayous. The 1864 Red River Campaign in Louisiana* (Brassey's, 1998), 172.

They left Grand Encore and arrived at Alexandria, Louisiana on April 25.[41] After a few hours of rest, the retreating army again continued at a hard pace through sweltering heat, down a level, dusty road along the Cane River. Late in the morning, the fatigue of the troops caused a halt. They rested for two hours, while the stragglers caught up and they only received a cup of coffee. At 1:00 P.M., they started again, trudging wearily though the village of Cloutierville, finally stopping after midnight. A member of the 116th New York stated, "It was a terrible march, trying to the utmost the endurance of every man. Scores were unable to keep up, and with an utter disregard of life, they fell out of the column unable to move further." Behind them, there was the constant sound of cannon fire.[42]

Saturday, April 23, 1864

Still continued our march. The rebs were following us as close, in fact- it was difficult to tell which way was our front, for the enemy were on all sides. Arrived at the crossing at 9 AM, found the enemy in force on the other side. They had a beautiful trap to lead us in. Their fortifications were so arranged as to rake us from all directions, in case we tried to cross. But instead of that we swam the river below and moved on them completely out flanking them.

---

[28] Compiled Records Showing Service of Military Units in Volunteer Union Organizations- Company E, 23rd Wisconsin, NARA M594, roll 201.
[39] William Riley Brooksher. *War Along the Bayous. The 1864 Red River Campaign in Louisiana* (Brassey's, 1998), 173-174.

161st NY- "We move out at daylight, and reach the ferry on Cane River at Monetts Bluff. This is a high precipitous bluff on the opposite bank of the river, they have four guns posted in plain sight which cover the large plain approaching the ferry for a long distance, higher up and further back, they have more guns scatted all along the line. They plant more than twenty guns we are told along the ridge masked by trees and shrubbery that are hiding a large force of the enemy. The division moves square against the bluff, but they cannot depress their guns enough to reach us, the shots go over us humming, our guns in the rear firing over us are making it very interesting for the battery immediately in our front, the regiment is waist deep in the waters of the swamp for a long time. A large force has gone up the river to another ford to try a flank movement while we hold them here in front." [43] The troops formed into a single line and slowly crossed the waist-deep river. A boat filled with noncommissioned officers who were trying to keep dry capsized, the troops were very amused as they watched as the officers flounder around trying to gain both footing and dignity. Once the troops crossed the stream, they struggled up a steep bank and sloshed through marshy undergrowth until they reached drier ground.[44]

Sunday, April 24, 1864

They now fell back we marched around and came to the old bridge, halted a few minutes and we were again ordered on. Again arrived at the pine woods. Marched till 11 at night and camped east of Bayou Rapids.

Monday, April 25, 1864

Continued our march through the pine forest. Old Gen A. J. Smith was bringing up the rear. He had heavy skirmishing with them every day. Arrived at Red River just before dark.

---

[30] Civil War Unit Histories, Part 3, The Union- Mid-Atlantic, *Roster and Monograph 161st Reg't, N.Y.S. Volunteer Infantry* by J. W. Merwin, 128.
[41] William Riley Brooksher. *War Along the Bayous. The 1864 Red River Campaign in Louisiana* (Brassey's, 1998), 179.

Tuesday, April 26, 1864

Still remain in camp. This is the first rest we have had for some time and is very acceptable to our poor sorefooted boys. Gen A. J. Smith's army is just passing. I presume they are going to the rear to rest a little. They have done bravely and earned a rest. Recd clothing and shelter tents for the Company from Lt. F. H. Lull.

Wednesday, April 27, 1864

Issued the clothing, camp garrison equipage. Just finished the clothing when the detail came for me as officer of the picket. I was posted on the Shreveport road with 52 men and three Sergts.1 Genl McClenard arrived this afternoon from Texas with the 1st Brig of the 1st Div and assumed command of his old ac. It is a beautiful night to stand picket, clear and moonlight. Stragglers from the Brig (cavalry) are coming in from the front and report that the enemy is advancing and our force falling back.

Thursday, April 28, 1864

Thursday morning has arrived bright and pleasant. As I was up all last night, I feel quite sleepy this morning. From the heavy firing in the night, I should think there was not skirmishing. We were relieved at 9 AM by a detail from the 1st Brig of the 1st Div. Returned to camp and found to my great pleasure that Capt Bull had returned to the Company, Genl McClenard having assumed command of the 13 AC, Capt Bull was relieved.

Friday, April 29, 1864

We changed our position today and now occupy near the center of our line in front of town of Alexandria. Our Reg connects on the right side with the 3rd Div Comd by Genl Cameron. We have thrown up very strange breastworks. All appears to be quite in front today.

Saturday, April 30, 1864

This has been quite a busy day. The Co was mustered for two month more pay. Next I made out the monthly report. Then the Maj informed us that the Pay Master would be here in the morning and pay off the Reg. So we had the Pay rolls signed. The next work was to make out the clothing receipt rolls.

Sunday, May 1, 1864

Maj Brigden made his appearance this morning with his old chest of green backs. Our Company was called up; first, but as "H" had to go on picket, he paid that Co first and our next. Heavy skirmishing today, there is now a rumor that the rebs have sank one of our gun boats. Just been ordered to march to the front at 1 PM. Marched up three miles in advance of our old position. Had a little skirmishing.

From May 1 to May 12 they stationed them near Alexandria, Louisiana performing picket and outpost duty.[45]

Monday, May 2, 1864

Still remained in the same line. All has been comparatively quiet in our front. Has been some fighting on our left today on the Opelousas road.

Tuesday, May 3, 1864

All is still quiet in our front. There is a little skirmishing. Our orders are just to maneuver around, hold our own ground, but not bring in a general engagement.

---

[29] Compiled Records Showing Service of Military Units in Volunteer Union Organizations- Company E, 23rd Wisconsin, NARA M594, roll 201.

Wednesday, May 4, 1864

Heavy skirmishing advanced the line of our Div. Just discovered that the rebs are on the north side of the Bayou. At 3 Oclock PM our Reg was called out to support the Pickets. Advanced the line of pickets one mile. Stationed them close, by the side of the Bayou. The rebs now open on our picket line with artillery. Our batteries return the compliment and soon dislodge the enemy.

Thursday, May 5, 1864

Our advance has driven the enemy back five miles. I was detailed to report to Rear Admiral Porter on the flag ship Cricket with 25 men. Went up the river on the Prt Hindman 15 miles after forage. Found Genl Taylor's army in force, fell back again to the rapids.

Friday, May 6, 1864

Arrived again at the rapids. Lt Pierce reported the result of our reconnoisance. We then landed and marched back to camp. I could not but regret that we could not remain the whole five days "which was the time for which we were detailed." We were used so very well while on the boat. Rejoined the Reg at noon.

Saturday, May 7, 1864

Ordered to march at 5 AM. Marched only five miles. Again formed in line. The 1st Div is two miles in advance. All has been quiet and upon the whole spent quite a pleasant day. The troops from the front came in and formed in the rear of our line at 11 PM.

Sunday, May 8, 1864

All is still again today. The 1st Div and 1st Wis battery moved out again to the front. Very strange moments. Just one month ago today we were having pretty serious times at Sabine Cross roads.

Monday, May 9, 1864

All is yet quiet the days pass tiresomely slow. Our sole object is just hold them here until our gun boats get below the rapids. Four of the boats went over last night, but the dam broke, thus preventing the remaining 6 from crossing.

161st NY- "April 30 work on the dam begins today, a large force of men is at work, felling trees, hauling brick and stone and a dam is being built on the lower fall, they are building a large crib out from the south bank. We fill it with anything that is heavy enough to sink, we are tearing down brick buildings for the brick and stone, and taking all the heavy machinery from the sugar mills and cotton gins for the same purpose, a wide span is left open between the wings that is to be filled by sinking large coal barges, the men have now been working a week. They have raised the water more than five feet at the upper falls, and three of the light-draught gunboats have passed the upper falls and are in the deep water above the dam, great crowds, not only of soldiers, but citizens also, line the banks watching the outcome. The troops have been at work constantly for eight days. One the morning of the ninth, the barge in the center broke out. The water went out in a raging torrent, but only a few of the boats were in readiness to take advantage of the rush, the Lexington, one of the large boats and the three small ones that passed the upper falls on the 8th. It was a moment of great anxiety and suspense, as the Lexington entered the swirl and rush of the water. I doubt if there was a person in all the thousands who lines the banks of the river watching, thought for a moment that she would go through the narrow shoot in safety, as she went over the rock her bow plunged downward. She was almost obscured from sight in the surge and spray of the foaming torrent, but as she rode into the waters below and was seen to be safe, the greatest cheer I ever heard went up from the crowd. It came alike from friend and foe. Three others followed quickly before the waters fell, but there were still eight more above the falls. Eight days work have been practically come to naught, there is a strong feeling against the navy, the men who have worked day and night for their salvation feel they should have been ready for any emergency, as it is, to save the larger part of

the fleet the army must do the work over again."[46]

Tuesday, May 10, 1864

Still remain in the same place. Expect to be detailed some time, yet on account of the dam breaking and preventing the gun boats from getting down. Our baggage was today put on board one of the transports ready to be sent down the river.

Wednesday, May 11, 1864

All remains quiet in front. They have succeeded in getting all the gun boats over the rapids, except four.

Thursday, May 12, 1864

Still remain in the same position. All the gun boats are now over and we shall probably leave soon. 4 PM detailed as officer of the picket. Extended the line 1 mile south west of camp. The reserve is at the old sugar house. The rebs ran up to the advanced post, our pickets fired on them. Rebs ran back in woods.

161st NY- "May 9 wing dams are being built at the upper falls, the regiment is building a large crib near the Spanish house, by superhuman exertions this new work is completed in three days and nights and the remainder of the fleet pass the falls in safety the 13th witnessed by an immense throng. The fleet is valued at four million, and was saved to the country by the indominatiable pluck and endurance of the army."[47]

---

[32] Civil War Unit Histories, Part 3, The Union- Mid-Atlantic, *Roster and Monograph 161st Reg't, N.Y.S. Volunteer Infantry* by J. W. Merwin, 129.
[33] Civil War Unit Histories, Part 3, The Union- Mid-Atlantic, *Roster and Monograph 161st Reg't, N.Y.S. Volunteer Infantry* by J. W. Merwin, 129.

Friday, May 13, 1864

Our Div was ordered to the ready to move at sunrise. Commenced marching at 4 AM. I was relieved from picket at 4 PM and rejoined the Reg. Marched 10 miles. Struck the river and camped for night.

As far as Fort DeRussy the march followed the bank of the river, so they could cover the withdrawal of the fleet of gunboats and transports against any possible attacks.[48]

They commenced the march to the Mississippi River and arrived at Morgansas Bend, Louisiana on May 22.[49]

Saturday, May 14, 1864

Commenced our march at 5 AM. Followed the river and guarded the train. The rebs commenced firing on our transport at 9 AM. The gun boats then opened upon them with shell grape and canister. Not much loss of life. Went into camp at 10 PM.

Sunday, May 15, 1864

Our Reg is rear guard the column commenced moving at 4 AM. Our Brig remained till noon, guarding the rear while the train crossed the Bayou Archafays. Had a skirmish in afternoon. Marched till 2 AM. And then slept till day light.

Monday, May 16, 1864

Resumed our march at 6 AM. Marched all day on a broad prairie. The rebs tried to capture our train. Had a heavy artillery fight in morning. Marched through some of the handsomest country in the US. Stopped at sundown to make coffee and rest. Rested till 10 PM and then resumed our march. Marched all night.

---

[40] Richard B. Irwin, *History of the Nineteenth Army Corps* (G. P. Putnam's Sons: New York, 1892), 344.

[30] Compiled Records Showing Service of Military Units in Volunteer Union Organizations- Company E, 23rd Wisconsin, NARA M594, roll 201.

161st NY- "In the afternoon we halted near a small stream of sparkling water, the first fresh clear water we have seen for over a month, the men break into one wild cheer and make a rush for the stream, canteens were filled and after a short rest the march is resumed and we camp at night along the road, am told we are eight or nine miles from the Atchafalaya."[50]

Tuesday, May 17, 1864

Arrived at daylight at a small Bayou where we made coffee and rested a few hours. Continued our march with skirmishing all day. Camped for the night at Brown Bayou and __ for the first time for several nights good nights rest.

Wednesday, May 18, 1864

Still remain on the Brown Bayou. Heavy cannoning and musketry in front. Genl Smith is evidently whipping the rebs. Our troops are now just returning from the fight. Have brought in 200 prisoners. And driven them (the enemy) six miles.

Thursday, May 19, 1864

Just received orders to draw one days rations and sixty round of cartridges. And be ready to march. Marched at 2 AM. Are now engaged in guarding the steamboat landing. Just below Sisumopas (?) on the Atchafalaya River. Bivouacked for the night on the Atchafalaya River.

Friday, May 20, 1864

Remained in the same position till noon. When then crossed the river by means of pontoon bridge constructed with steamboats and plank. Remained till 5 PM near the river and again resumed our march. Marched all night. Arrived at the mouth of Red River at 7 AM.

---

[35] Civil War Unit Histories, Part 3, The Union- Mid-Atlantic, *Roster and Monograph 161st Reg't, N.Y.S. Volunteer Infantry* by J. W. Merwin, 130.

The Atchafalaya was swollen to a width of six hundred or seven hundred yards by the back water of the Mississippi, and thus the floating bridge, which the year before was made by lashing together not more than nine boats, with their gangways in line, connected by means of the gangplanks and rough boards, now required twenty-two boats to close the gap. Over this bridge the troops took up their march in retreat. After A. J. Smith crossed the bridge it was broken up and the entire army marched for the Mississippi.[51]

Saturday, May 21, 1864

Continued our march towards Morganzas Bend. At 2 PM for some unknown reason our Div is ordered back to the mouth of the Red River. Arrived there at dark. And bivouacked for the night by the side of the Miss. Ordered to be ready to march at 3 AM.

Sunday, May 22, 1864

Resumed our march at an early hour. Arrived at Morganzas Bend at 2 PM. Found a large mail waiting for us. Received 8 letters form home. Again procured our tents and baggage from the boats and we enjoyed a comfortable nights rest.

They reached Morganzia on the 22, having marched, during the retreat, 175 miles.[52]

Monday, May 23, 1864

Still remain at the Bend. Spent the day in writing and attending to Co business. Had general inspection at 3 PM.

---

[43] Richard B. Irwin, *History of the Nineteenth Army Corps* (G. P. Putnam's Sons: New York, 1892), 346-347.

[51] E. B. Quiner, Esq., *The Military History of Wisconsin* (Chicago: Clarks & Co. Publishers, 1866), 717.

Tuesday, May 24, 1864

Received orders to be ready to march at a moments __. Turned over for transportation 2 Enfield Rifles, 1 Cartridge Box. Went on board the steamer *Kate Dale* at 5 PM. Rained hard, poor accomodations on the boat. Ordered not to sail until orders arrive from new Orleans.

Wednesday, May 25, 1864

Ordered to disembark. Left boat and marched Reg back to camp. The wagons and transportation of the 19 Ky 67 __ are loaded on the *Kate Dale*. Our Reg again embarked and at 6 PM started down the river for Baton Rouge. Arrived there at 10 PM. A detail of 90 men unloaded the freight at __ the Reg remained on board.

They debarked at Baton Rouge, Louisiana, where they were stationed, doing Garrison duty.[53]

Thursday, May 26, 1864

Another detail of 90 men and 2 commissioned officers called for to unload the steamer Pioneer. I am on duty with the detail. Reg disembarks marches ½ mile from the river and camps in a pleasant grassy place. The weather is exceedingly hot.

Friday, May 27, 1864

Spent most of the day in making out the muster rolls, which should have been done a month ago, but could not from the fact that were no blanks in the Reg.

Saturday, May 28, 1864

Co drill from 7 to 8. The Brig inspector came around at 8 and condemned 12 knapsacks, 12 haversacks and seven lanteens. Col Guppy arrived this afternoon also the rest of our recruiting Sergts and J. C. Wikoff with another mail.

---

[31] Compiled Records Showing Service of Military Units in Volunteer Union Organizations- Company E, 23rd Wisconsin, NARA M594, roll 201.

Sunday, May 29, 1864

This has been an exceedingly hot day. Have our hands full of business. Capt Bull made out his __ returns for the last Quarter of 1863. And we again commenced working on the muster and pay rolls.

Monday, May 30, 1864

Reveille at 5 AM. Worked on muster rolls till breakfast time. Co drill at 7 ½. Completed the rolls by 9. Co drill again at 4 PM.

Tuesday, May 31, 1864

Reveille at 5. Company drill at 5 ½. Company drill again at 7. Sergt Tyle's drilled the company while I made out the monthly returns. Brig drill at 5 PM.

Wednesday, June 1, 1864

Maj Greene ordered the regimental teamsters to haul cane for each company to make shade to protect them from the sun. Had the usual squad and Co drills in the morning. Company drill again in the afternoon.

Thursday, June 2, 1864

Reveille at 4, squad drill at 7. The company has fixed up a nice shade in front of their street.

Friday, June 3, 1864

The same routine of camp life. The usual drills.

Saturday, June 4, 1864

This has been a wet disagreeable day. Had no drills it being Saturday. The boys had a chance to wash their clothes.

Sunday, June 5, 1864

No drill today. Spent the day in writing and reading. Dress parade at 6 PM.

Monday, June 6, 1864

Turned over two Enfield Rifles for transportation. Took a memorundam receipt. Received notice that Samuel G. Rice is still in Genl hospital Recokuk. (?) Clothing account settled to 31 of Aug. Last paid by Maj Smith Feb 29 1864.

Tuesday, June 7, 1864

The transfered men from the 11 also the recruits left to join their Reg. Soloman Wiltrout left the Rifle I furnished him in place of the one he lost.

Wednesday, June 8, 1864

Rained hard in night. No drill this morning on account of it being so wet. Maj Greene is Post Officer of day which leaves the Reg in command of Capt Tolford. Dress parade at 6 PM conducted by Capt Bull.

Thursday, June 9, 1864

It has been found by careful inquires that the present cost of putting a Reg into the field aside from the government expenditures and boundries of all kinds at 15,000.

Tuesday, June 14, 1864

Maj Brigdon has just paid the Reg for the months of April and May. Had Company drill this afternoon. Brigade drill at 5 Oclock. Received orders to send in application for furloughs for 5 per cent of the Co.

Wednesday, June 15, 1864

Had Genl inspection at 10 AM. Sent in application for furlough for Corpl Webb and John F. Calkins.

Thursday, June 16, 1864

The usual morning drill. Grand review at 6 PM. The troops were reviewed by Genl Sickles the hero of Gettisburg.

Friday, June 17, 1864

Nothing of importance the usual drills and routine of camp life.

Saturday, June 18, 1864

No drill today. Company Ors thoroughly policed. Men all wash their clothes. Clean up their arms.

Sunday, June 19, 1864

Regimental inspection at 8 ½ Oclock. Capt Bull left for New Orleans. On duty as Officer of the day.

Monday, June 20, 1864

Company drill as usual. This is an intensely hot day. Afternoon drill dispensed with on account of the __.

Tuesday, June 21, 1864

The same routine of camp life. Company drill at 8. No drill this afternoon on account of the rain.

Wednesday, June 22, 1864

The same routine of camp life. As we are in garrison, performing picket and guard duty and having our usual drills comprises the sum of our employment. I shall therefor fill up the next few pages with some songs.

My Southern Sunny Home

1st Oh mother dear I have come home
    The home I loved so true
    But I'm unhappy all is changed
    Yet theres no change in you
    Each flower lifts it blushing face
    The birds are glad I've come
    My Souther Sunny Home

chorus
    My Home! My home my Southern sunny home
    Dear mother I've come home to die in my southern
        sunny sunny home

2nd It seems a few short years ago
    Oh we were happy then
    But mother dear Oh! Weep not now
    For will be glad again
    There is a place in yonder skies
    Where angels love to roam
    Where you and I are sure to find
    A brighter sunny home   Chorus

Just Before the Battle Mother

1st Just before the battle Mother
      I am thinking most of you.
      While upon the field we're marching
      With the enemy in view
      Comrades brave are round me lying
      Filled with thoughts of home and God
      For well they know that on the morrow
      Some will sleep beneath the sod

Chorus
      Fare well mother you may never
      Press me to your heart again
      But I will not forget my Mother
      If I'm numbered with the slain

2nd Oh I long to see you Mother
      And the loving ones at home
      But I'll never leave our banner
      Till the traitors all around
      That their cruel words we know
      By the help they give the foe

Chorus

3rd Hark I hear the bugles sounding
      Tis the signal for the fight
      Now may God protect us Mother
      As he ever does the right
      Hear the battle cry of freedom
      How it smells upon the air
      Oh yes we'll rally round the standard
      Or we'll perish nobly there   Chorus

Tuesday, June 18, 1864

The sun is extremely hot today. Reveille at 4½. The usual company drill at 6 AM. Day passes agreeably. Played a game of chess with the captain. Had the usual dress parade at 6 PM.

Wednesday, June 29, 1864

This has been a most beautiful day. I drilled the company at the usual hour. The Capt. went as usual to the Court Martial. And returned again in the afternoon the Court having dissolved. I was very glad to have the Capt. Come back and take charge of the company.

Thursday, June 30, 1864

This is an interesting day for us in camp- it being our usual muster day Col. Gill mustered us this morning. Had a little rain today- cool and pleasant.

Friday, July 1, 1864

Received several good loving letters from home. Amelia acknowledges the receipt of the draft I sent.

Saturday, July 2, 1864

Beautiful day. Capt. Bull is Div. Officer of the day. Having nothing of importance to attend to I devoted a little while to the study of chess. The Capt. is at home in evening and reads aloud from Shakespeare. Evening passed very pleasantly.

Sunday, July 3, 1864

Received another mail from the North. But I recd no letter this time. Returns of clothing, camp and garrison equipage.

Monday, July 4, 1864

One year ago today and we the dusty weary veterans of Genl. Grant who were made happy at the brilliant successes at Grand Gulf, Port Gibson, Raymond, Jackson, Champion Hills, Black River Bridge, again rejoiced at the surrender of Vicksburg after being under fire forty days and nights. Day passed very pleasantly very little disturbance in the Bay.

Tuesday, July 5, 1864

The day is very hot today- but a cool refreshing breeze occasionally makes it bearable. It is rumored today the Grant is in Petersburg. Picket today with 30 men and non commissioned officers. My post is on the clay cut road. Had a very pleasant time.

Wednesday, July 6, 1864

Relieved from picket at 9 AM by officer from Ind. Returned to camp and prevailed on the Col. To send out a team for bush for shade for the company. Teams returned with brush, erect a fine shade. Rumors extant that we are going down the river.

Thursday, July 7, 1864

Have had a fine rain- and the day is beautiful and cool. Every letter from the north mentions the extremely hot weather and no rain. Would to God that our farmers could have part of the rain that we are having here.

Friday, July 8, 1864

Received orders this morning to be ready to march at an hours notice. Embarked on the transport *Edward Walsh* for New Orleans. Nothing of importance occured on the way. But we have a decidedly pleasant time, spent the evening singing on deck. Arrived at New Orleans at 10 PM.

Saturday, July 9, 1864

Debarked at Algiers early in afternoon and encamped.

The regiment was encamped at Algiers, opposite New Orleans from July 8 to 26.[54]

Sunday, July 10, 1864

This is a beautiful day. Our camp is a fine one situated ½ miles from town on a fine clover field. Capt. Bull is at New Orleans.

Monday, July 11, 1864

The usual drills. The Reg is improving fast in drill and personal appearance.

Tuesday, July 12, 1864

Today we are brigaded with 99th Ill, 97th Ill, 21st Iowa. Col. Guppy commands the brigade in a Div. Commanded by Gen. McGinnis. Spent the day in New Orleans. Had good visit with Serg. Roche. Went all through The United States barracks is a splendid place.

Wednesday, July 13, 1864

Lt. Col. Gill and Maj. Greene have gone to the city to try and make a change in our fire arms viz exchange our Enfield Rifled Muskets for Springfield. I think this change was effected.

Thursday, July 14, 1864

Had a Genl. Inspection this morning by Capt. Mohr of 29 Wis and act inspector Genl. We condemned 25 guns and sets of accontrements for Co. "E."

---

[53] E. B. Quiner, Esq., *The Military History of Wisconsin* (Chicago: Clarks & Co. Publishers, 1866), 717.

Friday, July 15, 1864

Had the usual drill- immediately after drill had a Co. Inspection. Took an inventory of all the public property. Wikoff comes over from the city in evening but brings no mail.

Saturday, July 16, 1864

Co drill at 7 Am. Capt. procured a pass and has spent the day in New Orleans. The sun has been extremely hot all morning but in afternoon a fine breeze arose making it very pleasant. Spent the day in reading the tactics and playing chess.

Sunday, July 17, 1864

Procured a pass from the Col. and crossed the river to New Orleans to see Sergt. Hugh Roberts who was sick in St. Louis hospital.

Monday, July 18, 1864

No drill this morning, but several inspections by Capt. North 29th Wis. He condemns most of the guns recommends we change our Enfield Rifled Muskets for the Springfield.

Tuesday, July 19, 1864

Our new guns and accoutrements arrived today. The old Ordnance was properly turned over to each company commander and each Co recd a complete outfit of new guns and accouterments.

Wednesday, July 20, 1864

Drilled Co this morning in the skirmish drill. The Capt. has gone to New Orleans to turn over the old Ordnance to the ordnance depot.

Thursday, July 21, 1864

The sun has been extremely hot. Had a short drill in the skirmish drill.

Civil War Diary: Transcription 69

Friday, July 22, 1864

Nothing of importance. The same routine of camp life. The weather pleasant but hot.

Saturday, July 23, 1864

Had a short company drill. I was then detailed as officer of the guard. Received a mail one kind letter from sister Amelia.

Sunday, July 24, 1864

Relieved from guard at 9 AM. This has been a most splendid day such cool refreshing breezes. The splendid brigade band played for us on parade which went off finely.

Monday, July 25, 1864

Had a short Co drill this morning. The sun is extremely hot. But by keeping in the shade we can pass the time very comfortably.

Tuesday, July 26, 1864

The day has passed in the usual manner. Nothing of importance occurred til midnight when we received orders to get ready to move at a moments notice.

They embarked on the Transport *Jennie Rogers*.[55]

Wednesday, July 27, 1864

Packed up and at 3 Am struck our tents and moved to the landing. At 6 AM embarked on the Jennie Rogers and steamed up the river for Morgansias Bend. The day was fine and we had a most splendid time.

---

[32] Compiled Records Showing Service of Military Units in Volunteer Union Organizations- Company E, 23rd Wisconsin, NARA M594, roll 201.

They debarked at Morganza Bend, Louisiana and encamped.[56]

Thursday, July 28, 1864

Disembarked at Morganizia Bend one mile below the old camp that we occupied last May. All appears quiet at the Bend. The rumors in relation to the rebs being this side the Atchafalza river in large force is incorrect.

Friday, July 29, 1864

Several Regiment were sent out today to recouvitre. Had a skirmish with the enemy from the opposite side. The 19th Wis. lost several men. Capt. Bull has gone out tonight with 25 picked men from the Reg. to form an ambuscade and support the Pickets.

Saturday, July 30, 1864

The sun has been extremely hot today. Had our usual skirmish drill at 7 AM. The Capt. indicated all the commands by signs while we repeated by the chiefs of sections. Lt. Dickey of the 2nd Texas Cavalry visited us this morning. He is a Mexican and a most agreeable man. The Reg. was organized at Brownsville, Texas and the man are all from Mexico.

Sunday, July 31, 1864

Had our usual Sunday morning inspection. The arms are in most excellent condition. The Co. are proud of their new Springfield Rifles. Spent the day in reading and making out the monthly returns.

Monday, August 1, 1864

Another most beautiful day, but the sun is extremely hot. Had our usual skirmish in the morning. Inspection in the evening instead of retreat.

---

[33] Compiled Records Showing Service of Military Units in Volunteer Union Organizations- Company E, 23rd Wisconsin, NARA M594, roll 201.

Tuesday, August 2, 1864

The same routine of camp life after the usual drill. Played chess with Ford. Beat him twice out of three times. Inspection at retreat.

Wednesday, August 3, 1864

Skirmish drill at 7 AM. Spent the day in reading and playing chess. The mail packet and Greg Eugle arrived this evening with a mail, recd. Three good cheerful letters from home.

Thursday, August 4, 1864

No drill today. So the Col. sent out teams for brush and we have fixed up a fine shade in front of our tent. Inspection at retreat.

Friday, August 5, 1864

This has been an extremely hot day. But we have fine shade in front of our tents we can pass the time very pleasantly. Our friend Jacob C. Wikoff arrived from N. O. this evening with a large mail for the brigade. John Appley recd. a letter from the agent of scientific American informing him that his model was approved and he is sure of his patent. Cap. Bull has forwarded an application for a furlough for him.

Saturday, August 6, 1864

No drill today the companies are completing their shades, which add greatly to their comfort. Cap. Bull is relieved as brigade officer of the day at 7 AM. Spent most of the rest of the day in playing.

Sunday, August 7, 1864

This is a most lovely day, the sun is hot, but there is a fine refreshing breeze. Had the usual Sunday morning inspection at 8 AM. Spent the rest of the day in reading. The sutler has just arrived with a large stock of goods from N. O.

Monday, August 8, 1864

Very hot today no drill. Spent most of the day in playing chess and reading. Our Reg. is called for from our Brigade to go on a three days scout. The 99th Ill is the __ and reports at 9 PM at brigade Hqr with three days rations.

Tuesday, August 9, 1864

No drills this morning. Spent most of the day playing chess and reading. Recd. a mail bring the __ news that Newville was ours. Had surrendered with 44 pieces of artillery and 36 commissioned officers.

Wednesday, August 10, 1864

Had our usual skirmish drill at 7 AM. Lt. Dickey called upon us this afternoon, a very pleasant time he belongs to the 1st Mexican cavalry. The 35 Wis. arrived here this afternoon from St. Charles on White River they expect to go below.

Friday, August 12, 1864

Company drill at 7 AM. Had a visit from Lt. McCormick from the 35 Wis. he is quite an agreeable young man but his health being poor, is going home on leave of absence. Received a small mail from north. Spent the evening in playing chess.

Saturday, August 13, 1864

No drill today the men clean throughly their quarters and wash their clothes. Capt. is officer of the day. Dress parade at 7 PM.

Sunday, August 14, 1864

This is most beautiful day but very hot Co. Gill drilled the Reg. for the first time at 9 AM. At noon I was detailed as officer of the escort. Went 5 miles beyond out pickets to move a family inside our lines. Took dinner with an old planter. Returned our scout at sundown with plenty of chickens.

Monday, August 15, 1864

Company drill at 7 AM. Considerable rain today. No dress parade.

Tuesday, August 16, 1864

Rained greatly all day. But towards evening it cleared off just had Gen. inspection. The Div. inspector (Cap. Kenny) has condemned 2 knapsacks, 3 haversacks, 4 canteens and 3 shelter tents.

Wednesday, August 17, 1864

This is a most lovely day the sun is very hot but we have a fine refreshing breeze. Had our usual battalion drill at 7 AM. In afternoon George Nelling came up and made us a visit had a very pleasant time. He is clerking for Cap. Hull in the Post Commissary.

Thursday, August 18, 1864

Company drill at 7 AM. Dress parade at sundown.

Friday, August 19, 1864

Very rainy today. No drill. Spent the day in playing chess and reading.

Saturday, August 20, 1864

Received orders to be ready to embark at a moments notice for N. Orleans. Embarked on the transport Silver Wave at 2 PM and commenced our passage from the river.

The One hundred and sixty-first New York and Twenty-third Wisconsin Volunteers were to prepare to embark at a moment's notice for New Orleans, taking two days' rations. Transportation was to be provided that afternoon.[57]

---

[34] *The War of the Rebellion: A Compilation of the Official Records of the Union and Confederate Armies* (Washington: Government Printing Office, 1893), Series I-Volume XLI, Part II- Correspondence, Etc. Union- General Orders No. 27 p.781.

Sunday, August 21, 1864

Another fine day we have not made any great distance as we were detained last night. Arrived at Baton Rouge at daylight. The day has passed pleasantly and 11 PM finds us at the great commercial mart New Orleans.

Monday, August 22, 1864

Disembarked from the *Silver Wave* and embarked on the ocean steamer *Cahawba*. This is a most splendid vessel. Have excellent accommodations and all of gaily. Arrived at the mouth of the river at midnight and immediately crossed the bar and entered the Gulf.

Twenty-third Wisconsin and the One hundred and sixty-first New York Volunteers, were ordered to go by the steamer Cahawba, to Mobile Point and then to report to Major General Gordon Granger, commanding U. S. forces. [58] **The regiments have taken all their sick with them, some of them in such a condition that taking them beyond this place may not be advisable, and they suggested that a medical officer be sent to the Cahawba to inspect those sick and the men too feeble to travel transferred to a hospital in this city. The commanding officer also reported that they are entirely out of forage, and asked that twenty four hours' rations for twelve horses may be sent to the Cahawba. The commanding officer was to delay his departure as little as possible after they attended to these wants.** [59]

---

[35] *The War of the Rebellion: A Compilation of the Official Records of the Union and Confederate Armies* (Washington: Government Printing Office. 1893), Series I-Volume XLI, Part II- Correspondence, Etc. Union- Special Orders No. 105 p.799.

[36] *The War of the Rebellion: A Compilation of the Official Records of the Union and Confederate Armies* (Washington: Government Printing Office. 1893), Series I-Volume XLI, Part II- Correspondence, Etc. Union- Special Orders No. 105 p.802.

Tuesday, August 23, 1864

Passed Mobile Point at daylight and continued our course toward the Fort Gainley (?) and Morgan. At 6 AM arrived in sight of Faraguts (?). Blockading squadron the vessels appear to be close to Fort Morgan we form the impression that the fort has been taken. About 9 AM rec. a dispatch containing the glorious information that Fort Morgan surrendered to the United States forces at 4 AM and our vessel was ordered to enter the Bay by the main channel.

Wednesday, August 24, 1864

Disembarked this morning and landed on the Peninisula. Stacked arms close to the bay and made coffee. Moved again at 9 AM. Went into camp about 2 miles below the fort. Found the 29th Wis. here, two officers from the 20th came down and spent the afternoon with Capt. Bull. They told us all about their recent exploits in Texas and here.

Thursday, August 25, 1864

Our Reg also the 161rd NY, 77 Ill, 96 Ohio, 34 IA and 67 IN embarked on the boats, the object of the expedition was to take possession of Cedar Point which was done without opposition. Took possession of the fort. Had a fine super of oysters taken from the bay where they are very plentiful. The mosquitoes are so troublesome, slept very little.

On the 25 of August they sent the Thirty-Fourth, with four other regiments, on tin clads to Cedar Point to capture Fort Powell but found they had evacuated it. Here we spent two never to be forgotten days. Our movements stirred up the mosquitoes. At midday, under a broiling sun, they gathered in clusters on our clothing, and regardless of heavy woolen shirts and blouses drew forth our life's blood. At night we put up our little mosquito bars, built a smudge at both head and feet, lit our pipes and tried to sleep. These long-billed galli-nippers bit as if they never before had tasted Yankee blood. They provided the most horrid oaths ever listened to, but heeded neither man's cries, prayers nor execrations. [60]

Friday, August 26, 1864

Had nothing to do today. So I spent the day in roaming about the Point. Visited the fort which is a very formidable one. Captain Bull arrived this evening the transport Thomas. Had another fine oyster supper.

They remained at camp at Cedar Point, Alabama until September 2.[61]

Saturday, August 27, 1864

This has been a very busy day moved our camp to the other side of the beach which is a much better position. I am just detailed as officer of the Picket. Have 24 men and 2 non commissioned officers. Rained very hard at night. Mosquitoes very troublesome.

---

[36] Civil War Unit Histories, Part 4, The Union- Midwest and West, *The Thirty-fourth Iowa Regiment Brief History* (Des Moines: Watters-Talbott Printing Co., 1892) p.24-25.
[37] Compiled Records Showing Service of Military Units in Volunteer Union Organizations- Company E, 23rd Wisconsin, NARA M594, roll 201.

Sunday, August 28, 1864

Another beautiful day. Brought in a colored family that had run away from the rebs at Mobile, he reports that flour is $300 per bl, corn $15 per bu. They are in great fear of our forces. The boys had a fine time fishing. Had another drenching rain in the evening. Relieved at dark by Lt. Frost.

Monday, August 29, 1864

This is a most beautiful day but very hot. After transacting what little camping business I had on hand, I got a skiff and went out on the beautiful bay to fish with Capt. Bull and several others. Had pretty good luck came in at noon. Spent afternoon playing chess.

Tuesday, August 30, 1864

Commenced making out the muster rolls. Finished the roll then went fishing, had fine luck caught some splendid cat fish. Came in at noon, had our excellent dinner of fish. Made out another roll. Detailed at 4 PM as officer of the fatigue. Worked 2 hours on rifle pits on left of fort, was then relieved and marched to camp.

Wednesday, August 31, 1864

This is a busy day. The first thing on the program is out usual muster. My CO was mustered first at 5 AM. Next made out my monthly returns. In evening transport *Kate Dale* arrived from N. Orleans, bringing a mail. Jacob Wikoff brought the mail. Ordered to be ready to embark for Morganza.

The One hundred and sixty-first New York Volunteer Infantry and Twenty-third Wisconsin Volunteer Infantries were relieved from duty with the U. S. forces at Mobile Bay, and immediately embarked for Morganza, Louisiana. The quartermaster's department furnished the necessary transportation. They were to have twenty days' rations, heading to the mouth of White River, where the troops will go into camp.[62]

Thursday, September 1, 1864

Ready with two days rations cooked. I am detailed as officer of fatigue. Have 26 men and 2 non commissioned officers also 2 fine __. Move the brigade stores from the landing, store them on transport N. W. Thomas. Finish at 9 AM brigade embarks 23rd Wis on *N. W. Thomas*, 161 N. York on *Kate Dale*, detained till morning on account of the barge being a ground.

Friday, September 2, 1864

Our steamer is still at the pier tugging away at the heavily laden barge, assisted by a gun boat. See rebel scouts riding about Cedar Point visiting the fort and our old camp. At 10 AM succeed in clearing the barge assisted by the rising tide. Steamed over to Fort Powel. Ran a ground and had to remain till morning.

They embarked the *N. W. Thomas* and went to Morganza, Louisiana where they arrived September 8.[63]

---

[38] The *War of the Rebellion: A Compilation of the Official Records of the Union and Confederate Armies.* (Washington: Government Printing Office,1893), Series I-Volume XLI, Part II- Correspondence, Etc. Union- Special Orders No. 113 p.931; *The War of the Rebellion: A Compilation of the Official Records of the Union and Confederate Armies* (Washington: Government Printing Office, 1893), Series I-Volume XLI, Part II- Correspondence, Etc. Union, 952..

[39] Compiled Records Showing Service of Military Units in Volunteer Union Organizations- Company E, 23rd Wisconsin, NARA M594, roll 201.

Saturday, September 3, 1864

Succeeded in getting off about 8 AM. Steamed over to Fort Morgan, distance 16 miles. Visited the fort which is formidable __. Found the 20 Wis encamped here. Left at 4 PM and ran to for Gaines at which place arrived at 5 PM. Found our suttler Wm. Greene waiting for us with a good stock of goods. Tied up for night, men allowed to go ashore and cook supper.

Sunday, September 4, 1864

Steamed over to Fort Powell and again ran a ground. Unfortunately in having a poor pilot. Got clear at 7 AM with the assistance of the steamer Planter. Made poor progress only making 56 or 61 miles.

Monday, September 5, 1864

Again __ in the Miss. Passed fort Jackson and Phileps at 2 PM.

Tuesday, September 6, 1864

Arrived at New Orleans at 5 AM. Boat remains all day men allowed to go ashore. Leave at 7 PM for Morganza. Capt. Bull left us on leave of absence.

Wednesday, September 7, 1864

Arrived at Morganaza at 2 AM. Landed below the fort and the 96 Ohio debarked. Again steamed up the river a mile above the fort and debarked. Went into camp in the old camp of 29 Wis.

Thursday, September 8, 1864

Mistake on previous page. Debarked this morning and went into camp.

Friday, September 9, 1864

Still remain at Morganza. Recd a mail. Recd one letter from home. Forwarded blank return vouchers to Capt Bull. Recd from Lt. F. H. Lull acting QM 23 Wis. 7 prs pegged shoes, 26 prs socks, 11 shirts, 8 prs pants, 4 prs drawers, 6 rubber blankets, 2 knap sacks, 1 haversack, 2 canteen, which I issued to the members of Co "E".

Saturday, September 10, 1864

Moved camp about ½ mile lower down the levee near the rest of our brigade. Boys all took hold with energy and we soon had a good, comfortable camp.

Sunday, September 11, 1864

The usual Sunday inspection at 8 Oclock- has been an extremely hot day. Wm Greene the suttler came up from N. Orleans today with a stock of goods.

Monday, September 12, 1864

Detailed as officer of Picket at 7 AM. My post was at the river. Arrested several stragglers and took in some contraband goods during the day. Officer of the day made his usual visit at 6 PM. Some firing during the night. Relieved at 7 AM.

Tuesday, September 13, 1864

Turned over my contraband goods to Adj. Genl. Worked hard all day at Co business. Had battalion drill at 5 PM.

Wednesday, September 14, 1864

Officer of the guard today which duty was light and did not interfere with CO business. Battalion drill at 5 PM.

Thursday, September 15, 1864

Had dress parade at 8 AM. The Reg made a fine appearance. Recd another mail one letter from sister Emili. Spent the day in transacting CO business.

Friday, September 16, 1864

Dress parade at 8 AM. Did a little Company writing. Rebel Cavalry made a dash upon our __ post. Killed two of our men, wounded several and captured 30. Our Reg unpredictably ordered out on an expedition. Marched 16 miles camped or rather bivoucked for the night on the new Texas road.

Guppey's troops marched in support of Colonel Davis, with the One hundred and sixty-first New York, Lieutenant-Colonel Kinsey commanding, and the Seventy-fifth and Ninety-second U. S. Colored Infantry; the last two named regiments reporting to him under their brigade commander, Colonel Frisbie. They marched nineteen miles during the night, and two miles further than was necessary, owing to want of exact information by the guide. After correcting his position, they went into camp at the head of Bayou Letsworth, on the ground where their men had been captured that morning. Colonel Davis was going down this bayou toward Simsport, and our camp was within three miles of the rear of his column at the time of our halt, but Guppey had not established direct communication with him.[64] They went on a scout in the direction of the Atchafalagua river and marched 25 miles and returned the next day.[65]

---

[40] *The War of the Rebellion: A Compilation of the Official Records of the Union and Confederate Armies* (Washington: Government Printing Office, 1893), Series I-Volume XLI, Part 1- Reports, No. 2, Operations in the Vicinity of Morganza, La., *Report of Colonel Joshua J. Guppey,* 804-805.

[41] Compiled Records Showing Service of Military Units in Volunteer Union Organizations- Company E, 23rd Wisconsin, NARA M594, roll 201.

Saturday, September 17, 1864

Resumed our march at 7 A.M.. Arrived at Atchafalya River at 10 A.M.. Found the rebs had improved their time and made their escape on the other side. Saw a few scouts on the opposite side. Our battery fired a few shells. We then commenced our march back. We marched 15 miles and bivouacked for the night.

In the morning they followed Colonel Davis's force seven miles toward Simsport, when they met a messenger from Colonel Davis informing Guppey that the rebels had got across the river and that the cavalry was on its return. He halted till Colonel Davis came up, and his information confirming what they had told him, viz, that it was twenty-five miles to Morgan's Ferry by any practicable route from where we were, and the object of my joining Colonel Spicely having ceased to exist by the escape of the rebels to the north side of the Atchafalaya, Guppey decided to return to Morganza. Colonel Davis gave him 200 calvary and preceded him with the rest of his force on the return. They marched back about fourteen miles and went into camp at 5:30 p.m., having made less than twenty-four hours.[66]

Sunday, September 18, 1864

Reveille at 4 AM. Breakfast at 4½. Commenced our march at 5 AM. It was hot and not having marched any distance for some time, we were all foot sore. Arrived in camp at 11 AM. Louis had a fine fish ready for us for dinner. Spent the afternoon in writing some letters.

Monday, September 19, 1864

Dress parade at 8 AM. Spent most of the day in reading and writing. Battalion drill at 4 PM. Capt. Schlick drilled the Reg as Co. Hill was unwell.

---

[42] *The War of the Rebellion: A Compilation of the Official Records of the Union and Confederate Armies* (Washington: Government Printing Office, 1893), Series I-Volume XLI, Part 1- Reports, No. 2, Operations in the Vicinity of Morganza, La., *Report of Colonel Joshua J. Guppey*, 804-805.

Tuesday, September 20, 1864

Reveille at 6 AM. Dress parade at 8 AM. Col Hill commanded the Reg Battalion drill at 3 PM. Had a fine drill. Recd orders at 8 PM to be ready to march at 11½ and start at midnight to Atchafalya River. Had a tedious march all night.

They went on a scout to the Atchafalagua River, sixteen miles, which they reached on the next morning and returned September 23.[67]

Wednesday, September 21, 1864

Arrived at the river at 2 Am and a tired set of men we were found no rebs this side. Made our coffee, and then I had a good sleep.

This morning they came into camp at Morganza, marching about ten miles. Guppey's command suffered no loss while out, but many men are very footsore. That morning, while Colonel Frisbie was with the rear guard and he was at the head of the column, many men of the Ninety-second Colored Infantry broke from their ranks and commenced stealing poultry. When they advised him of their actions, he ordered them to stop pillaging. The Seventy-fifth Colored Infantry is an excellently behaved regiment and he admired their good behavior while the Ninety-second was straggling about houses and yards this morning. The lieutenant-colonel of the Seventy-fifth seems to be an excellent disciplinarian and he did not have any complaints with the Ninety-second, except the acts of pillage, and Colonel Frisbie assures him that they would properly deal with the guilty ones. Guppey was reluctant to mention the matter, that "no imputation may rest on my own character as an officer." [68]

---

[43] Compiled Records Showing Service of Military Units in Volunteer Union Organizations- Company E, 23rd Wisconsin, NARA M594, roll 201.

[44] *The War of the Rebellion: A Compilation of the Official Records of the Union and Confederate Armies.* Washington: Government Printing Office, 1893, Series I-Volume XLI, Part 1- Reports, No. 2, Operations in the Vicinity of Morganza, La., *Report of Colonel Joshua J. Guppey,* 804-805,.

Thursday, September 22, 1864

Still remain on the river. We sent out foraging parties from each Reg in the brigade. The boat was put in my charge which I kept plying to and from taking over the boys and bringing them back with their loads of sweet potatoes, beef, mutton, and chickens. Turned boat over at night to Col Kensey of the 161 New York. Slept Beautifully at night in the old store.

Friday, September 23, 1864

Reveille at 5 AM. Had breakfast and received orders to march forth. We commenced our march back to Morganza at 7 AM- rained making roads very muddy. Arrived at our old camp at 4 PM. Found all right, but there had been no mail nor Pay Masters.

Saturday, September 24, 1864

Reveille at 5 AM. Had the Co quarters thoroughly policed. Spent the day in doing some Co business.

Sunday, September 25, 1864

Reveille at 5 PM. Inspection at 8 AM. Spent most of the day in reading and writing. Received a mail in afternoon. Several letters from home. Dress parade at 5 ½. Spent the evening in answering letters.

Monday, September 26, 1864

I had the Co property inspection this morning. Had 15 shelter tents, 14 haversacks, 5 knapsacks and 8 canteens condemned. Spent most of the day in doing company business. Battalion drill at 5½ PM.

Tuesday, September 27, 1864

Picket officer today. My detail consisted of five non commissioned officers and seventeen men. I was on the river front. Had a very pleasant time. Arrested a smuggler in the afternoon trying to smuggle a large amount of contraband articles through the picket lines.

Wednesday, September 28, 1864

Relieved from picket at 7 ½ AM by Lieut Frost. Arrived in camp at 8 AM. Found Reg just falling in for dress parade. Took my Co on parade. 9 AM detailed as officer of the guard. Rained most of the day. Spent most of the time in making out my inventories and inspection reports of Camp and Garrison equipage.

Thursday, September 29, 1864

Dress parade at 8 AM. I was relieved from Guard at 9 by Lieut Frost. Spent the morning in posting up the morning report book. Had battalion drill at 4 PM. Spent the evening in making out the monthly return and in writing to the captain.

Friday, September 30, 1864

Had dress parade at 8 AM on the new parade ground north of camp. Received a mail on letter from Annie. Had a fine battalion drill this afternoon.

Saturday, October 1, 1864

As this is Saturday we had no drill but gave the men a chance to clean up throughly for the inspection tomorrow. Dress parade at 5 PM. Spent the evening in writing.

Sunday, October 2, 1864

Regimental inspection at 8 AM in light marching order. The Col expressed his entire satisfaction at the appearance of the Reg. In the afternoon received orders that we should embark at daylight the next morning on an expedition to Bayou Sera, the object of which was simply to cause diversion and hold what rebs might be at this point so that to favor another expedition that was starting, higher up on the river.

Monday, October 3, 1864

Reveille at 3 ½ AM. Breakfast at 4. Started for transports at 5 AM. 23rd was embarked at 7 on the *Ohio Belle*, the 1st La and Nebraska, 161st New York on the Ill debarked at Bayou Sera at noon. Marched 2 miles and filed into a beautiful grove and stacked arms. And remained all night, in the meantime a force of cavalry was sent out to scout through the county. Slept on the __ of the house at this place.

They embarked on the steamer *Ohio Belle* and went to Bayou Sara, Louisiana. They debarked and marched two miles to St. Francisville, where they remained until the next morning.[69]

Tuesday, October 4, 1864

Breakfast at 4 AM. Commenced our march at 5 AM. Marched to Jackson distanced 13 miles without opposition. I took dinner with the old priest. Remained till 3 PM during which time did some good foraging. Marched back 2 miles, crossed the Bayou and bivuacked for the night. During the night the rebs received reinforcements from Clinton and moved right down to the Bayou.

In the morning they marched to Jackson and encamped at night two miles south of the town.[70]

Wednesday, October 5, 1864

Considerable picket firing during the night, and at daylight the rebs commenced shelling us. Killed one man in Co "C" with first shot. Our battery returned the compliment with good effect. Commenced our march back to the river the enemy following us closely. Attacked us again as we were crossing an open field. Had heavy artillery duel. Corp Jones of Co "G" was killed several others wounded. Arrived at the river and embarked for Morganza arrived at Morganza at 6 PM.

---

[45] Compiled Records Showing Service of Military Units in Volunteer Union Organizations- Company E, 23rd Wisconsin, NARA M594, roll 201.

[46] Compiled Records Showing Service of Military Units in Volunteer Union Organizations- Company E, 23rd Wisconsin, NARA M594, roll 201.

John G. Norton
2nd Lieutenant, Company I, 23rd Regiment Wisconsin Infantry
credit: Robert C. Grossman Collection, USAMHI, Carlisle, PA

In the morning a heavy force of the enemy attacked them, which fought them the entire distance back to St. Francisville, but company E sustained no loss. They returned the same evening to Morganza.[71]

Thursday, October 6, 1864

Again in our old camp at Morganza, which seems very much like home. Recd from Lt. L. H. Lull 3 prs boots which I issued to Sergt Horton, Quigley and Dickinson.

Friday, October 7, 1864

Had a very cold night last night. Received orders to have the company in good order for Genl inspection. Received a mail two letters from home. The Brigade Quarter Master received the clothing, camp and garrison equipage.

Saturday, October 8, 1864

I was detailed as officer of the picket today. But Lieut Norton took my place so that I could attend to issuing the clothing. Received another mail and my invoice from Capt Bull of ordinance and ordinance stores.

Sunday, October 9, 1864

Regimental inspection in __ marching order. Reg made a fine appearance and Col Hull congratulate each Co Commander on the fine appearance of his Co. Another mail 2 letters from home. Dress parade at 5 PM.

Monday, October 10, 1864

Recd orders to be ready at 2 PM for Genl inspection. 1st orders countermanded. Ordered to be ready to embark with 5 days ration and 100 Rds cartridges. Embarked at 3 PM on transport the N. W. Thomas and commenced steaming up the stream.

---

[47] Compiled Records Showing Service of Military Units in Volunteer Union Organizations- Company E, 23rd Wisconsin, NARA M594, roll 201.

They embarked on the transport *Illinois* and ascended the Mississippi above the mouth of Red River, where they debarked on the western side.[72]

Tuesday, October 11, 1864

The object of the expedition was to put a stop to the rebs receiving cattle out of the interior of the country and swimming them across the river. Arrived at the point at 2 AM. Debarked at daylight. The calvary was sent out on a scout and the Infty kept at the boat. Cav returned at dark, found no cattle. We then marched out on another scout. 9 PM bivouacked for night.

Wednesday, October 12, 1864

Reveille at 4 AM. Commenced our march at daylight- struck on the tail of large herd of cattle- followed them till dark. Found the rebs had succeeded in getting them across Red River. 7 PM commenced our march back to the boats. Marched 9 miles and bivouacked for the night by the side of a large bayou.

Thursday, October 13, 1864

Commenced our march at daylight. Arrived at the boats at 9 AM. Found our camp equipage and sick had been moved up from Morganza and we were ordered to White River. Embarked as soon as we arrived on the transport Baltic. Soon were steaming up the river.

They marched thirteen miles on a scout and returned the next day, embarking on the transport Baltic and went to the mouth of the White River, Arkansas where they camped. They were transported 860 miles and marched 136 miles, a total of 996 miles.[73]

---

[48] Compiled Records Showing Service of Military Units in Volunteer Union Organizations- Company E, 23rd Wisconsin, NARA M594, roll 201.
[49] Compiled Records Showing Service of Military Units in Volunteer Union Organizations- Company E, 23rd Wisconsin, NARA M594, roll 201.

Friday, October 14, 1864

Still continue our course up the river. The weather is pleasant. The 1st La and 161st Reg are a fine gentlemantly lot of fellows.

Saturday, October 15, 1864

The weather is very cold today. I can say that I desire the change of climate at this season of the year. Arrived at Vicksburg at noon. Debarked and cooked three days ration, while the steamer was throughly cleaned. Embarked again at 7 PM and continued our course up the river.

Sunday, October 16, 1864

Still continued our course up the river. Nothing of importance occured. Purchased a fine turkey, which we had for dinner.

Monday, October 17, 1864

Arrived at White River, landing at 10 AM. Debarked at noon and went into camp in a large cotton field which was just ready to pick rather a ___ joke on the cotton.

Tuesday, October 18, 1864

Spent the day in fixing up our camp. The boys have fixed up very comfortably. Cheering news comes from the north in the relation to the election in Ohio and Indiana. If our friends will only be faithful and do their duty at the pools and put down the firing in the rear we will attend to matters in the front.

Wednesday, October 19, 1864

Spent the day in our nice camp. At 4 PM the Col calls for the Co Commanders. Ordered us to have our companies ready to embark at daylight. I had the cooks cook two days rations. Embarked at 6 AM on the steamer *Ellwood.* Orders countermanded and we debarked and returned to our old camp. Captain Bull arrived this evening on the steamer *Ida Handy*. I am officer of the Picket.

Thursday, October 20, 1864

This is a fine pleasant morning with the exception of it being rather cold. I was relieved this morning by Lieut Jolley. Came into camp at 8 AM with a good appetite for breakfast and enjoyed myself with the Captain it seemed so good to have him back again.

Friday, October 21, 1864

Detailed again as officer of the picket. As the other white Reg have left it makes the picket duty heavy for our Reg. We have 75 men, 17 non com officers and two commissioned officers detailed for the picket this morning. I had charge of 7 posts in the right of the line.

Saturday, October 22, 1864

Relieved this morning by Lieut Frost. Had Genl inspection at 3 this afternoon. The inspector was old Major from the regular army. The inspection was through.

Sunday, October 23, 1864

No Sunday morning inspection. Captain Bull is detailed with fifty men to go on a scout on the other side of White River. I am alone this evening. Recd a mail from home. One letter from Amelia. 11 PM detailed with 12 men and 3 non commissioned officers as an escort for transport Liberty up White River. Went on board *Liberty* at midnight.

Monday, October 24, 1864

Left the mouth of White River at daylight and steamed pleasantly up the river. Had a most agreeable let off passengers on board, the steamer was heavily loaded with government stores besides having in tow an enormous barge containing 300 tons of commissary stores. Ran a ground on sand bar at 4 PM. Steamer *Commerical* passed up at 5 PM but could not assist us.

Tuesday, October 25, 1864

After tugging away all night at the barge without success the Capt concluded to leave her in my charge with my fifteen men. She is leaking very fast. The boys are working hard at the pumps, she will go down by midnight unless lightened by another boat. 9 PM the transport Harry has just arrived sent from the mouth by Genl Reynolds. Put in the steam pumps and soon had her nearly dry.

Wednesday, October 26, 1864

The men are all still busy loading the Harry. Put in 200 tons. Three of my boys have just gone across the river in the __ and killed a beef. We have now an abundance of fresh meat of the finest quality. 9 PM the gun boat Cricket No. 6 has just come down, the Capt. has agreed to lay and guard us a few days.

Thursday, October 27, 1864

This is a must beautiful morning we are waiting patiently to see a friendly steam make its appearance on the bend of the River. PM The Tycoon has first come down from Duvalls Bluff but as she was loaded could not assist us.

Friday, October 28, 1864

6 AM transport *Rose Hamilton* and *R. B. Hamilton* have just passed up both having an escort from our Reg the 1st in command of Capt Sumner and the other in charge of Sergt Cary. It is lonesome here, but we have an excellent base of supplies, any amount of the boys are in excellent spirits and are faring well.

Saturday, October 29, 1864

Crossed the river with four of my boys for a hunt. Had fine success today killed three beef cattle. On our return found the steamer *Florence* had come down for a load of our freight. Lieut Norton was there with his escorts from the Reg. I divided the beef with his boys. Had supper on the Florence and slept there.

Sunday, October 30, 1864

The steamer *Florence* left early this morning with her second load for the Bluff. I had nothing to do so I went over to the gun boat and spent a good part of the day. 4 PM the transport *Delaware* had just passed.

Monday, October 31, 1864

This is another fine day. We are looking very hour for the Liberty to return. 3 PM transport *May Duke* has just arrived leaving us a barge to load. Says the Liberty was at the Bluff when she left. 6 PM *Liberty* has just arrived.

Tuesday, November 1, 1864

Price in his raid through Ms destroyed __ $ 4/5-000, Washington $300000 in Iron __ and Pacific Railroad $70000. Murdered citizens committed outrages to horrible to be recorded.

Wednesday, November 2, 1864

Arrived at the mouth of White River. Found the Reg embarked on a transport. Genl Dennis orders me to go on the Liberty as far as Helena. Took a vote of the crew and passengers, for curiosity, the result was 240 for Lincoln, 19 for McClallan and 19 neutral.

Thursday, November 3, 1864

Arrived at Helena at 10 AM. Found that we were to move into the quarters built by the 6th Minnesota. Genl Buford offered me to place a guard over the camp and prevent the removal of any property not strickly regimental. Our Reg arrived at 11 PM.

Friday, November 4, 1864

Moved into our new quarters which are decidedly comfortable. Spent the day in cleaning up.

They debarked at Helena, Arkansas where they remained November and December.[74]

Saturday, November 5, 1864

This has been a beautiful day. The camp is all alive the boys are fixing up their quarters in fine style. All seem anxious to remain here for the winter and are willing to prove by their good conduct that they are as worthy of the place as any other.

Sunday, November 6, 1864

Our Reg does the Picket duty today. The detail consists of 5 com officers, 19 non com officers and 75 men. The guard mounting took place in front of Genl Buford Head Quarters, which was gone through with a very creditable style.

Monday, November 7, 1864

I have been quite busy all day in making out my returns of clothing, camp and garrison equipage. Quite rainy and very muddy. This is a very disagreeable place in wet weather.

Tuesday, November 8, 1864

This has been a most beautiful day, and the muddy roads are drying fast. Recd a mail 2 letters from home. The election passed off harmoniously and resulted as follows, 320 for Lincoln to 20 for McClellan. Every man in CO "E" voted with the straight-nation ticket.

Wednesday, November 9, 1864

Our Reg furnished the Picket today 70 men, 21 non com officers and 5 com officers. My third of the line was on the Helena road near the brick kiln. All was quiet in the picket line. The officer of the day and visit the line at 11 AM and at midnight.

---

[50] Compiled Records Showing Service of Military Units in Volunteer Union Organizations- Company E, 23rd Wisconsin, NARA M594, roll 201.

Thursday, November 10, 1864

Relieved from Picket at 9 AM. On my arrival at camp found the Capt had drawn a fine lot of clothing for the Co which we proceeded to issue.

Friday, November 11, 1864

This is a clear pleasant day. Each Reg is improving this fine weather in fitting their winter quarters. Gen Buford and his At Genl visited our camp this afternoon.

Saturday, November 12, 1864

Made our my returns of ordinance and forwarded them to Ordinance officer. Dress parade at 5 PM, drew new clothing and the Reg presents a fine appearance.

Monday, November 14, 1864

The regular routine of camp life nothing exciting occured.

Tuesday, November 15, 1864

Reveille at 6 AM. Spent most of the day in studying and bookeeping.

Wednesday, November 16, 1864

This has been a most disagreeable day very rainy. Maj Greene passed up the river this PM on transport __ Stockney which landed and we went down to see him. His health is very poor has a leave of absence of 20 days.

N. B. Buford stated that the removal of the Twenty-third Wisconsin from Helena, Arkansas, before the return of the Sixth Minnesota will leave this post almost destitute of white troops. He requested that the Twenty-third Wisconsin be permitted to remain here until the Sixth Minnesota arrives.[75]

Thursday, November 17, 1864

Still very rainy a good time for indoor employment. Spent the day in reading one of Coopers works. Spent the evening playing chess with Lt Atkinson.

Friday, November 18, 1864

Detailed this morning as officer of Picket. It is a very rainy most disagreeable day. My post is on the Little Rock Road. Rained all night making it severe for the out posts.

Saturday, November 19, 1864

Relieved this morning by the 60th Colored Infty. Arrived in camp at 10 AM found to my surprise that Capt Bull had rec his commission of Lieut Col of the 5 Wis. He has started for Alexandria, VA, this evening. I am very sorry to lose the Capt from the Co.

Sunday, November 20, 1864

This has been a most disagreeable day very rainy and muddy. Kept in my quarters all day and spent my time in reading and writing. Rec a mail one letter from Amelia.

Monday, November 21, 1864

Clear and cold this morning. Our camp is drying up very fast. The boys have been working hard all day improving their quarters, which are now very comfortable.

---

[51] *The War of the Rebellion: A Compilation of the Official Records of the Union and Confederate Armies* (Washington: Government Printing Office, 1893), Series I-Volume XLI, Part IV- Correspondence, Etc.- Union p.582-583.

Tuesday, November 22, 1864

This has been a very pleasant day with the exception of being cold. I am detailed as officer of the __ party which went out after wood. The teams hauled in 9 fine loads of wood.

Wednesday, November 23, 1864

Clear and cool this morning. Had Regimental inspection this afternoon and the inspector examined my Co books and papers. Genl Buford arrived here from White River this afternoon.

Thursday, November 24, 1864

Reveille at daylight. Guard mounting at 8 AM. Lieut Stanley is officer of the guard. I spent most of the morning in playing chess with Lieut Stanley. Recd a mail also an extension of furlough for Hugh Roberts.

Friday, November 25, 1864

Reveille at daylight- the usual guard mounting at 8. Lt Akinson is officer of the guard. Spent most of the morning in playing chess with him and the afternoon was spent in attending to Co business.

Saturday, November 26, 1864

On Picket today my post is on the Little Rock Road. The roads are very muddy and but little travel. Several loads of cotton and some merchandise passed through the lines.

Sunday, November 27, 1864

Relieved this morning at 9. Very wet and muddy in camp. Our Chaplain preached this evening.

Monday, November 28, 1864

Officer of the covering guard detail consisted of 20 men, 10 with axes and 10 with guns. Went out on the Little Rock Road hauled in 9 fine loads of wood. Arrived in camp at 4 PM. Dress parade at 5 PM.

Tuesday, November 29, 1864

This has been a most beautiful day. Company drill this morning. Dress parade at 5 PM. Spent the evening in making out the monthly return.

N. B. Bufford stated that General Reynolds had been in Helena since he left Memphis, and directed that the Twenty-third Wisconsin should remain at that post until the Sixth Minnesota relieves it. He has also applied to General Canby for instructions to transfer the Sixth Minnesota to Brig. General A. Shaler's brigade, leaving the Twenty-third Wisconsin in my command. The Sixth Minnesota is the largest regiment.[76]

Wednesday, November 30, 1864

On Picket. Had guard mounting in front of the Genl's at 8 AM. I am on the right of the line today my post which is the reserve is on the Sterling (?) Road considerable travel and the day passed pleasantly.

Thursday, December 1, 1864

Relieved this morning at 9. Spent the day in attending to some company business. Turned over all my tents.

Friday, December 2, 1864

Detailed this morning as officer of the covering party. Went out about 4 miles on Little Rock Road. Arrived in camp just in time for dress parade.

Saturday, December 3, 1864

Reveille at daylight. Spent the day in posting up my company order book.

---

[52] *The War of the Rebellion: A Compilation of the Official Records of the Union and Confederate Armies* (Washington: Government Printing Office, 1893), Series I-Volume XLI, Part IV- Correspondence, Etc.- Union p. 712.

Sunday, December 4, 1864

Detailed at Hd Qrs found it was a mistake, marched back to camp and dismissed my men. 9 AM detailed as body guard for the Genl reported on the Bells Hamilton. Steamed down as far as Triers Point. Brought up prisoners and contrabands.

Monday, December 5, 1864

Arrived in camp from our trip up the river at 2 AM. Been off duty the rest of the day of a ___. Detailed to night as officer of the Picket tomorrow.

Tuesday, December 6, 1864

Reveille at daylight. Guard mounting at 8 ½. I have charge of the center division on the brick kiln road, quite a nice house for the reserve. A most beautiful day and we had a very pleasant time. Col Hill officer of the day visited us there once during the day.

Wednesday, December 7, 1864

We were relieved this morning at 9½ by the Corps. Arrived in camp at 9½.

Thursday, December 8, 1864

Guard mounting at 8½. I am officer of the guard today. It is a very cold disagreeable day. Received a mail several letters from Wis.

Friday, December 9, 1864

Not on duty for a ___. It is a cold disagreeable day and I spent most of the time in my quarters.

Saturday, December 10, 1864

Detailed as officer of the guard. Guard mounting at 8 ½ AM.

Sunday, December 11, 1864

This has been a most winterly day for this climate there is a little snow on the ground and extremely cold. Spent most of the day in putting wood in the stove and stuffing up the cracks.

Monday, December 12, 1864

Detailed this morning as officer of the picket with Lieuts March and Norton. I take the centre division and guard the road near the brick kiln. Guard mounting at Genl Buford Hd Qrs. Arrived on picket line at 9 AM. Day passed pleasantly.

N. B. Buford told Major General J. J. Reynolds that he had your verbal order to retain the Twenty-third Wisconsin at this post until the return of the Sixth Minnesota relieved it, but as time enough has elapsed for the return of that regiment and it has not come, he suggests that the Twenty-third Wisconsin be retained here and other dispositions be made of the Sixth Minnesota. He further stated that if the regiment is taken away from here and none sent in its place that he will be left with an inadequate force. The Twenty-third Wisconsin, though much smaller than the Sixth Minnesota, is well disciplined and he would prefer to have it.[77]

Tuesday, December 13, 1864

Relieved this morning by the 60th Colored. Arrived in camp at 10 AM with an excellent appetite for my breakfast. Recd a mail notice of extention of Private Loren B Francis furlough.

Wednesday, December 14, 1864

Quite warm and pleasant today. Dress parade at 5½ PM.

---

[53] *The War of the Rebellion: A Compilation of the Official Records of the Union and Confederate Armies* (Washington: Government Printing Office, 1893), Series I-Volume XLI, Part IV- Correspondence, Etc.- Union p. 834-835.

Thursday, December 15, 1864

Our Reg furnished the picket this morning. Guard mounting at 8½. Liets Duncan and Atkinson and Stanley are officers of the picket. Maj Genl Gilmore arrives here inspects the fortification. Our Reg is ordered to be ready to fall in for inspection if he should visit the camp.

Friday, December 16, 1864

This has been another wet disagreeable day. Spent most of the day in writing in the evening moved over into Lt Frost and Norton tent which is very comfortable. Vacated my room to my Co who now occupy the whole house (four rooms). And are now very comfortable.

Saturday, December 17, 1864

This has been a wet disagreeable day. Spent most of the time in playing chess. Played chess in the evening with Capt Dunham and Lieut Marsh.

Sunday, December 18, 1864

Our Reg furnished the picket this morning. The officers detailed are Lieuts Atkinson, Norton and Jolly.

Monday, December 19, 1864

Embarking on steamer Dove at 9 Am. Arrived at the mouth of the White River at 5 PM. Delivered my dispatches to Capt Noble and the Stock and Q. M. stores were unloaded as soon as practicable.

Tuesday, December 20, 1864

Finished up my business for the General at the mouth of the river, started in our return at 3½ AM. Arriving at Lacina at 9 Am at Is 66 at 1 PM, Gillins landing at 1½, Island No. 63 at 5 PM where we remained all night. I got all the information I could at each of these places in relation to cotton and cotton traders.

Wednesday, December 21, 1864

Steamed up again at 3 AM arriving at Helena at 8 Am. Arrived in camp just as the picket were going out. Recd a mail this morning good news from home and Sherman. Also from Thomas in Tennessee.

Thursday, December 22, 1864

Detailed as officer of the guard. Spent most of this day in playing chess. Received glorious news of Genl Thomas victory in Tenn capturing 5000 rebels and 30 pieces of artillery.

Friday, December 23, 1864

This has been a rainy disagreeable day. I spent most of the day in playing chess with Lieuts Marsh and Atkinson. Detailed this evening for picket tomorrow.

Saturday, December 24, 1864

This is a cool pleasant frosty morning. Guard mounting at 8 ½ AM. I command the 2nd Div and am stationed upon the Brick Kiln Road. Capt Duncan is seiguir officer of the line and my post at 11 AM with Adj Dussen.

Sunday, December 25, 1864

Relieved this morning by the 60 US Colored Inf. Rather a disagreeable day for Christmas. Had a fine Wis turkey for dinner. Spent most of the afternoon in playing chess.

Monday, December 26, 1864

This has been quite a pleasant day. The boys are all exulting over the great success of Genl Thomas.

Tuesday, December 27, 1864

Detailed as officer of the Picket. Guard mounting at 8 AM. I command the 3rd division stationed on the Little Rock Road. Had a most pleasant time on Picket.

Wednesday, December 28, 1864

Relieved this morning at 9. Arrived in camp at 10 AM. Played a game of chess with Capt Duncan and Lieut Atkinson. Maj Greene arrived from Wis this evening was heartily welcomed by the whole Reg.

Thursday, December 29, 1864

Officer of the guard. Guard mounting at 8 Am. Been busy all day making out the muster rolls.

****

Example page of diary

Friends and Acquaintances

The following is an alphabetical listing of the men mentioned in the diary. In 1862 the company clerk, did not follow regulations, as he did not enter the physical description of the men who mustered in on the regimental descriptive rolls. He described the later recruits in 1864. [78]

Appleby, John Francis   Private - Company E, 23rd Wisconsin

He was born 23 May 1840, in Hampton, Westmoreland County, New York, the son of James Appleby and Jane Wishart. In 1845 he moved to Wisconsin with his parents and settled on a farm near Palmyra. In 1858, while working on his stepfather's (Marshall Newell) farm in Iowa County, he invented the basic knotting device that was to become the foundation for all farm binding machinery. On 15 August 1862, James M. Bull enlisted him for three years at Madison, as a private in Company E, 23rd Wisconsin. His home was Mazomanie, Dane County, Wisconsin. He mustered on 30 August 1862, single, age twenty-two and mustered out 4 July 1865. At the time he enlisted, he was 5'6", with a light complexion. When he returned home, he brought rings for each of his girlfriends that he had carved out of rubber buttons. He married Anna Delight Spink on 16 October 1866 in Madison. She was born 11 February 1842 in Kane County, Illinois the daughter of Soloman Lewis Spink and Roxanna Barrus. They had three children Ruby Grace born 16 April 1868 in Mazomanie, Dane County; John Roy born 17 July 1874 in Rockton, Winnebago County, Illinois. James Percy born 23 July 1875 in Augusta, Eau Claire County, Wisconsin.

While in the army, Appleby invented a cartridge magazine and a needle gun. The government rejected the gun and Appleby sold the patent cheaply. The weapon was used extensively in the Prussian army. After leaving the service he lived in near Mazomanie, Wisconsin, where in 1867 he tested his first grain binder unsuccessfully. He moved to Beloit in the early 1870's, where he continued his experiments in the farm machinery shop of Charles H. Parker and Gustavus Stone. In 1874 he

---

[78] *The Company Clerk: showing How and When to Make Out all the Returns, Reports, Rolls, and Other Papers, and What to do With Them* by Capt. August V. Kautz (Philadelphia: J. B. Lippincott & Co, 1863), 30-32.

developed a successful wire binder, but was refused financial support because of farmer resentment against the use of wire binding. In that same year he returned to Mazomanie to construct self-rake reapers, forming the Appleby Reaper Works. After a few months he returned to Beloit where, with the backing of Parker and Stone, he perfected a successful twine binder. They issued patents in 1878 and 1879. William Deering, of Gammon and Deering, purchased a license to build the binders and large-scale production began. Within a few years the twine binder had completely replaced the unpopular wire binders and Appleby's design became the basis for machines produced by the McCormick, Champion and Osborn companies. In 1881 he sold his patent interests to the Campion Machine Works in Springfield, Ohio and moved to Minneapolis until 1892. The twine binder, called a "self-binder," enabled the farmers to expand their wheat crops. In 1882, the McCormick Company, having turned from wire binders to twine binders, sold more than fifteen thousand twine binders. The twine binders with their automatic knotters made possible the rapid extension of the wheat belt. Large scale farming became common practice in those areas. One farm near Casselton, North Dakota, had sixty self-binders as early as 1882. They granted the first shop-right to Hoover, Allen and Gable of the Excelsior Harvest Works at Miamisburg, Ohio. They built one each for several other firms and sold licenses to manufacture under a royalty of six dollars on each machine. In 1882 the McCormicks paid them thirty-five thousand dollars for the right to manufacture twine binders. They sold out the entire plant to one of the larger firms and laid the foundation of what later grew to be the International Harvester Company. He worked for the Deerings for many years, but he retired after it was consolidated into larger firms. He was living in Minneapolis in 1889 when he attended the second reunion for the 23rd Wisconsin at Milwaukee, 28 August 1889. He filed for an invalid pension on 29 December 1899. His disability was due to diarrhea, hemorrhoids, rheumatism and failing eye sight. In 1901 he was 61 years old, 5' 7 ½," 160 pounds, light complexion, hazel eyes, brown hair, his pension was $6.00 per month. He continued to work on various inventions and patented a horse-drawn cotton picker. In 1917, when he was seventy-seven years old they described him as a stocky build old gentleman whom they might have taken to be twenty years younger. His face was described as looking like General Grant's if he had worn whiskers. He moved to Chicago, Illinois in November 1911, then to Davenport, Iowa and back to Chicago where he died 8 November 1917. In 1927, the Smithsonian Institution, United States

National Museum, Division of Mineral and Mechanical Technology requested information about Appleby. They were compiling a biographical file on pioneer inventors, industrialists and engineers. The original model of his twine binder is in the museum of the State Historical Society in Madison.[79]

John Francis Appleby

---

[79] Wisconsin Adjutant General, Regimental Descriptive Rolls 1861-1865, 23rd Infantry, Company E. (FHL #1311689); National Archives, Washington D.C., Pension File: John F. Appleby, Company E, 23rd Wisconsin Infantry, invalid pension filed: 29 Dec 1899, application # 1241246, certificate #999116, filed in Illinois; *Dictionary of Wisconsin Biography* (The State Historical Society of Wisconsin: Madison, 1960) p. 13-14; Industrial Hemp Farming- History & Practice; http://www.druglibrary.org/schaffer/hemp/indust/INDHMPFR.HTM; Ancestral File version n419 submitted 1997 by Mrs. Joanna Nicklin of Creve Coeur, MO; International Genealogical Index version 4.01; Civil War Unit Histories, Part 4, The Union- Midwest and West: Regimental Histories and Personal Narratives. *The Survivors of the Twenty-third Regiment Wisconsin Volunteer Infantry*, 1889; Wisconsin Magazine of History v. 1, No.3, March 1918, p.333; Wisconsin Magazine of History v. 5, No. 2, 1921 p. 207; Wisconsin Magazine of History v 10, No. 1, Sep 1926 p. 35-41; Wisconsin Magazine of History v. 10, No. 3, Mar 1927, p. 310-314..

Armstrong, James   First Sergeant, Company E, 29th Wisconsin

On 13 August 1862, D. J. Wells enlisted him for three years at Fox Lake, as first sergeant, in Company E, 29th Wisconsin. He mustered in 27 September 1862, at Madison, 22, single, black eyes, black hair, light complexion, 6', clerk. His home was Fox Lake, Dodge County. He was a quarter master when he was discharged on 2 August 1863 at Vicksburg.

He married Elizabeth J. Smith on 20 September 1866 at Commerce. She was born 16 October 1843 in Commerce, Michigan. *He contracted a cough and bronchial trouble while in the army, which soon settled on his lungs and in the year 1865 had fir first hemorrhage and from that time grew gradually worse until the time of his death.* James died 13 May1871 in Boscobel, Wisconsin and was buried in the Fox Lake Cemetery. The cause of death was lung disease, usually called consumption. Lizzie married second Frank B. Hoadley. After James died, she lived in Commerce, Michigan and taught music until she married Frank Hoadley. They lived in Detroit until he died there on 20 September 1895. According to their son, Fred J. Armstrong, Mr. Hoadley committed suicide, *but not from domestic causes or trouble.* Mr. Hoadley was buried in Elmwood Cemetery. After his death, Elizabeth lived in Detroit for 18 years, then moved in with her son, Fred J. Armstrong. Fred J. Armstrong was born 4 July 1868.[80]

---

[80] National Archives, Washington D.C., Pension File: James E. Armstrong, Company E, 29th Wisconsin Infantry, Lizzie J. Hoadley, widow pension filed 3 September 1897, application #661349, certificate #846420, filed in Wisconsin.

Atkinson, Alexander First Lieutenant, Company A, 23rd Wisconsin

He was born 24 October 1839 at Florence, Boone county, Kentucky. He served three months in company K, 1st Wisconsin Infantry, he then mustered in as second lieutenant on 25 August 1863 at Madison, single, age 25. He was first Lieutenant, commissioned into Company A, 23rd Wisconsin on 9 December 1863. When he mustered, his home was Pleasant Springs, Dane County. He was taken a prisoner at Battle Carrion Crow Bayou on 3 November 1863 and exchanged on 26 December 1863. He saw the following actions: Chickasaw Bayou; Port Gibson; Champion Hills; Black River Bridge; Siege of Vicksburg; Jackson; Carrion Crow Bayou; Sabine Cross Roads. He mustered out on 4 July 1865.

He married Tempie Wright on 8 Jan 1867 at Milwaukee, Wisconsin in the Methodist Episcopal Church. They had two children; Millie Bell was born 13 September 1868, died 21 August 1869 and Grace Blanche born 15 September 1877 died 6 December 1880. In 1879 he was living at 1217 Dodge Street in Omaha, Nebraska, where he was a merchant. He filed for an invalid pension on 2 November 1881. In 1898 both of their children were dead, but they had his youngest sister's child, Henry George Atkinson Black, living with them. Henry's mother died in childbirth and they took him in when he was a day old. He was born 15 February 1888. In 1890 Alexander was living at 316 N. 20th Street in Omaha, Douglas, Nebraska when he applied for an increase of his pension. He stated that *he incurred injury to his head due to an explosion well known in history as the Mobile Explosion. The ammunition had been concentrated in warehouses on the Bay for storage or shipment. An explosion occurred, which shattered and overturned several buildings and caused great loss of life.* He was a quartermaster of the camp of distribution. At the instant of the explosion, he was on duty in his office, within two blocks of one warehouse that exploded. Jacob C. Wycoff, formerly a private in Company C, 23rd Wisconsin, claimed that he was *acting as a clerk to Lieutenant Atkinson at the time of the explosion. He gave a great deal of irrelevant information regarding the account of the explosion and doesn't state definitely that Atkinson was injured at that time. At the time the case was in the field for special examination, the witness was insane and it was deemed unnecessary to obtain a disposition from him.*

His first wife, Tempie died in Boston, Massachusetts on 12 October 1900, of pernicious anemia, and she is buried at Mt. Auburn Cemetery in Cambridge. Alexander married second, Margaret J. Lindsay of Washington, D.C. on 2 July 1901 at St. Andrew's Episcopal Church in Washington, D.C. Alexander died in Boston on 2 October 1919 of hypertrophy of the prostate, and is buried at M (?) Cemetery in Boston. Margaret J. Atkinson filed for a widow pension on 6 November 1919.[81]

Alexander Atkinson
(Signature.)

---

[80] Wisconsin Adjutant General, Regimental Descriptive Rolls 1861-1865, 23rd Infantry, Company A. (FHL #1311689); National Archives, Washington D.C., Pension File: Alexander Atkinson, Company A, 23rd Wisconsin Infantry & Company K, 1 Wisconsin Infantry, invalid pension filed: 2 November 1881, invalid application #432471, certificate #247425, filed in Nebraska. Margaret J. Atkinson, widow pension filed 6 November 1919, application #1148456, certificate #882201, filed in Massachusetts.

Buford, Napoleon Bonaparte   Major General

He was born into Kentucky's plantation society on 13 January 1807 in Woodford County, Kentucky. He graduated from West Point in 1827, then studied law at Harvard. One of his classmates, thirty-five years later wrote (Buford) *is as good a fellow as ever lived, and most devotedly my friend; a true Christian, a true soldier, and a gentleman, every inch of him.* He served eight years in the artillery and was an assistant professor of natural and experimental philosophy at West Point in 1834-1835. He married Sarah Childs and the first of their two children was born in 1832. He resigned from the army in 1835 and returned to Kentucky, where he was a resident engineer of the Licking River Improvement Project. While he was there, his family, which included his father, stepmother and three half-brothers, moved from Kentucky to Rock Island, Illinois. After completing his work he joined his family where he and his half-brothers established an iron foundry that became the J. I. Case Company. They ran a pork house, shoe factory, grocery, coal company and ship's chandlery. He operated the Bank of the Federal Union, was the director of the Rock Island Line and president of the Peoria & Rock Island Railroad. He lobbied the U. S. Congress to establish an arsenal at Rock Island, founded the first gas company in the area and was in the Illinois legislature. His wife Sarah died in the late 1850's and he married Mary Ann Greenwood, a widower, in 1859. In 1861, the default of Southern bonds financially ruined him. He then entered the Union army when he was fifty-four years old, as colonel of the 27th Illinois volunteers. His assignments included: colonel, 27th Illinois (10 August 1861); commanding Flotilla Brigade, Army of the Mississippi (24-26 April 1862); commanding 1st Brigade, 3rd Division, Army of the Mississippi (26 April-25 June and 20 September-1 November 1862); major general, USV (29 November 1862); commanding District of Eastern Arkansas, 16th Corps, Army of the Tennessee (19 September 1863-6 January 1864); and commanded the District of Eastern Arkansas, 7th Corps, Department of Arkansas (6 January -6 August, 28 September -7 October 1864, and 10 October 1864-9 March 1865). He fought under Grant at Belmont, under Pope at Island # 10, and under Rosecrans at Corinth. In the last two he directed a brigade. He served in early stages of the Vicksburg Campaign, but his appointment as a major general was not confirmed by the Senate and it expired on 4 March 1863. Napoleon Bonaparte Buford, the half-brother of Gettysburg hero John Buford held the rank of major general for only a few months. During the later part of the war he commanded in eastern Arkansas, with headquarters at Helena. He was breveted major general and was mustered out on 24 August 1865. He was Superintendent of the Federal Union Mining Company of Colorado from June to December 1866. He served as special U. S. Commissioner of Indian Affairs, February to September 1867. He was the superintendent for inspecting the Union Pacific Railroad from September 1867 until March 1869, when the road was completed. His health began to fail in 1882, due to old age. On 24 March 1883 he fell unconscious and moved to a hospital, where he never regained consciousness. He died 28 March 1883 in Chicago, Illinois and is buried in Rock Island, Illinois beside his father and Sarah and Mary at the age of 76. [82]

Napoleon Bonaparte Buford

---

[81]*The Union Army* (Broadfoot Publishing Company; Wilmington, NC, 1998) vol. 8:42; American Civil War Site, http://www.;civilwarhome.com/nbufordbio.htm; *Civil War Times*, story by Benton McAdams, THE OTHER BUFORD A Gettysburg hero's exuberant half-brother lived life with an independent spirit his commanders came to hate; Karen Walker of Pagosa Springs, Colorado; George W. Cullum, *Biographical Register of the Officers and Graduates of the U.S. Military Academy at West Point, N.Y.* (Boston and New York; Houghton, Mifflin and Co., 1891) p.389-390; *Ezra J. Warner, Generals In Blue. Lives of the Union Commanders.* (Louisiana State University Press. 1964) p. 53-54.

Bull, James M. Lieutenant Colonel - Company B, 23rd Wisconsin

He was born 21 October 1839 in London, England, the son of James and Lydia Bull. He was Lieutenant Colonel of 5 and K, I and B, 11 and 8, 23 Wisconsin Infantry. The Governor of Wisconsin commissioned him on 16 August 1862. He mustered in Company E, on 30 August 1862 at Madison, age 23, his home was Middleton, Dane, Wisconsin. On 15 July 1863 he requested a leave of absence for twenty days to attend to *important business connected with his aged fathers' estate and by which he may save him his homestead.* He needed to take home his brother-in-law who was severely wounded at Vicksburg on May 22. The surgeon said he could not live in that climate. They had excused him from duty only five or six times, since he mustered in 1861. They took him a prisoner at Battle of Carrion Crow Bayou on 3 November 1863 and exchanged 26 December 1863. Engagements: Chickasaw Bayou; Arkansas Port; Port Gibson; Champion Hills; Black River Bridge; Siege of Vicksburg; Jackson, Mississippi and Carrion Crow Bayou, Louisiana. He was living in Stillwater, Minnesota in 1889. He attended both reunions of the 23rd Wisconsin, the first at Madison 15-16 September 1886 and the second at Milwaukee, 28 August 1889. He filed for an invalid pension on 15 November 1892, due to disability, listing repture or hernia, piles and kidney and liver troubles. He died 1 November 1909 in Gentry, Benton County, Arkansas, of pneumonia. His physician, Clinton A. Rice stated that James was *a moral and religious man, addicted to no vicious habits whatever*. He married Martha Ann "Mattie" Sanford on 24 August 1862 at Madison. She was born in Ogle County, Illinois on 2 July 1840 and they didn't have any children. His widow, Mattie Sanford Bull, filed for a widow pension on 19 November 1909. [83]

---

[82] Wisconsin Adjutant General, Regimental Descriptive Rolls 1861-1865, 23rd Infantry, Company E. (FHL #1311689); Ancestral File, version n419, submitted 1991 by Anne Sanford; Service Records, National Archives, Washington D.C.; National Archives, Washington D.C., Pension File: James M. Bull, 23rd Wisconsin Infantry, invalid pension filed: 15 November 1892, application #1137660, certificate #1009992, filed from Minnesota. Mattie S. Bull filed widow pension 19 November 1909, (application #930750, certificate #674,663, filed from Arkansas; Civil War Unit Histories, Part 4, The Union- Midwest and West: Regimental Histories and Personal

Butler, James O.   Private - Company E, 23rd Wisconsin

On 16 January 1864, J. G. Tyler enlisted him at Arena, for three years, as a private in Company E, 23rd Wisconsin. He mustered in on 19 January 1864 in Madison. He was 24, blue eyes, black hair, 5'5", fair complexion. They took him a prisoner at Sabin Cross Roads, Louisiana on 8 April 1864 and taken to Camp Ford Tyler, Texas. He transferred to 35th Wisconsin on 21 June 1865 and mustered out on 4 July 1865 in Mobile, Alabama. He applied for an invalid pension on 12 February 1882, being disabled due to chronic diarrhea and disease of the lungs while he was a prisoner of war.

He married Mary Ann 1860 in Dane County, Wisconsin. He had four children; Edgar born February 1867, Ann Maud born 19 July 1871, Christopher M. born 16 October 1872, Myra M. born 28 March 1875. In 1887 he was living in Clarion, Wright County, Iowa. In 1889 he was living in Clarion, Iowa. He attended the 23rd Wisconsin's reunion in Madison, 15-16 September 1886.[84]

James O Butler

Narratives. *The Survivors of the Twenty-third Regiment Wisconsin Volunteer Infantry*, 1889.

[83] Wisconsin Adjutant General, Regimental Descriptive Rolls 1861-1865, 23rd Infantry., Company E. (FHL #1311689); National Archives, Washington D.C., Pension File: James O. Butler, Company E, 23rd Wisconsin Infantry, invalid pension filed: 12 Feb 1882, application #561906, certificate #351615; Civil War Unit Histories, Part 4, The Union- Midwest and West: Regimental Histories and Personal Narratives. *The Survivors of the Twenty-third Regiment Wisconsin Volunteer Infantry*, 1889.

Calkins, John Franklin

He was born 20 December 1829 in Steuben County, New York, the son of John Calkins and Ruth Crawford. On 14 August 1862, James M. Bull enlisted him for three years at Mazomanie, as a private in Company E, 23rd Wisconsin. He mustered in 30 August 1862 in Madison. He was married, age 32, he served with his brothers Anson, Jerome and Stephen. He mustered out with the company on 4 July 1865 at Mobile, Alabama.

At age 53 he was 5' 10", light complexion, brown hair, hazel eyes. His wife, Abigail Wells was born 2 September 1835 at Hillsdale County, Michigan. They married on 21 May 1854 in Arena. They had the following children: Franklin Welles Calkins was born 5 June 1855 in Arena, Wisconsin and Jerome Burton born 1867. John and Abbie left Wisconsin for western Iowa on 8 September 1865. While they were in winter quarters, they were told of the Spencer Grove, which was a grove of large trees. During the winter the men went to the area, where they were *so pleased with country they decided without delay to locate there. Each made his selection for a homestead, went into the grove, cut logs for the houses they intended to build, then waited the coming of spring. They moved to this new location, the south half of section 18 in May....In their eager desire to do some breaking of sod, these men put cabins of small logs covering them with slabs of elm bark. They wrote to relatives back home* [Arena, Wisconsin area] *greatly in praise of the new country urging them to come west also.*

Franklin Welles Calkins, John and Abigail's son, spent his boyhood in the upper Missouri country and for ten years he was a plainsman and mountaineer. He attended the Iowa Agricultural college in 1876; taught school and read law for the next three years. In 1880 he began contributing stories of adventure and sketches of western life and character in the Youth's Companion and other publications. He is the author of *My Host the Enemy and Other Tales: Sketches of Life and Adventure on the Border Line of the West* (Chicago: Fleming H. Revell, 1901) which was 7¾x5 and *Two Wilderness Voyages: A True Tale of Indian Life* (Chicago: Fleming H. Revell, 1902.) More than three hundred of his serials and short stories have been published.

John filed for an invalid pension on 24 February 1883. They were living in Spencer, Iowa in 1889 and he attended the 23rd Wisconsin's reunion in Madison on 15-16 September 1886. In 1897 he was 5'9", 144 pounds, 67 years. Then he was receiving $16 per month for chronic diarrhea and disease of the rectum and indigestion, and diabetes the result of stomach and bowel trouble. James M. Bull said that *on or about the 10th of January 1863 while in the line of duty he contracted chronic diarrhea and indigestion under the following circumstances. We marched from Milliken Bend to Dallas Station Louisiana a distance of about 35 miles in nine hours and the next day marched back again over the same ground. He was one of sixteen out of seventy to come into camp at night, the others being exhausted and unable to keep up. The road being muddy, and the weather cold, and stormy. About a week after the forced march Calkins was in the battle of Arkansas Post and stood out all night without fire, blankets or any protection. He was exposed to the cold and wet while in an exhausted condition. The next night they detailed him to take care of the wounded and was not released for 36 hours. He was without proper food or rest. The said claimant was also with us at Young's Point, a very wet and unhealthy location, for about six weeks and was sick all the time we were there.* His widow, Abigail filed for her widow pension on 21 February 1898. Abigail Welles Calkins and her son, Jerome Burton Calkins are buried in the Calkins family plot at the Lake Elsinore, California Cemetery.[85]

---

[84] Wisconsin Adjutant General, Regimental Descriptive Rolls 1861-1865, 23rd Infantry, Company E. (FHL #1311689); National Archives, Washington D.C., Pension File: John F. Calkins, Company E, 23rd 23rd Wisconsin Infantry, invalid pension filed: 24 Feb 1883, application #481318, certificate #292517, filed from Iowa. Abigail Calkins filed widow pension 21 Feb 1898, application #670809, certificate #469952, filed from Wisconsin; Civil War Unit Histories, Part 4, The Union- Midwest and West: Regimental Histories and Personal Narratives. *The Survivors of the Twenty-third Regiment Wisconsin Volunteer Infantry*, 1889. Kenneth W. Calkins of Golden, Colorado; *Herringshaw's Encyclopedia of American Biography of the Nineteenth Century, p. 185;* Canda Mitchell , web site (no longer available), Anson Miller Calkins was her great-grandfather; Carl Jerome Calkins, great grandson of John F. Calkins.

Cameron, Robert Alexander   Brigadier-General

He was born 22 February 1828 in Brooklyn, New York and lived there until 1842, when he moved to Valparaiso, Indiana. He graduated at the Indiana medical college in Chicago in 1849 and studied at the Rush medical college in Chicago. He practiced medicine and in 1857 he purchased the Valparaiso *Republican* newspaper. In 1860 he was elected to the Indiana Legislature, where they knew him as an active Republican leader. They also described him as a ready debater, forcible and argumentative, able, honest and fearless. He was a member of the Republican convention that first nominated Mr. Lincoln for the presidency. When the war broke out, he raised a company in two days and he mustered in on 17 April 1861 as captain in the 9th Indiana volunteers. He became lieutenant-colonel of the 19th Indiana Infantry in the same year and in 1862 made colonel of the 34th then promoted brigadier-general of volunteers in August 1863. He commanded the 13th army corps after General Ransom was wounded in the Red River expedition of 1864. Louisiana renamed half the parish of Sabine to "Cameron" after *the gallant General who so bravely defended the rights of the loyalists in the dark days of the rebellion.* During one of his campaigns, through exposure and exhaustion, he lost his eyesight, and for nearly two years he was totally blind. After the war he became a noted land speculator in Colorado, founding Greeley, Manitou and Colorado Springs. They appointed him the warden of the Colorado penitentiary in 1885 and in 1888 he became commissioner of the Denver, Texas & Fort Worth railroad. He was quietly following his favorite study, fruit, on his fruit farm at Canon City when Texas called him to take the position of commissioner of emigration for that road. He was about six feet tall and weighted more than 200 pounds. He died 15 March 1894 in Carson City, Colorado. [86]

---

[85]*The Union Army* (Broadfoot Publishing Company; Wilmington, NC, 1998) vol. 8:48; *The National Cyclopaedia of American Biography.* New York: James T. White & Company, 1897; James F. Willard, *The Union Colony at Greeley, Colorado 1869-1871*, Boulder, 1918 p.244-245; Obituary *Rocky Mountain News*, 16 March 1894 p.6c.6.

Robert Alexander Cameron

Carey, William   Corporal - Company A, 23rd Wisconsin

On 14 August 1862, W. F. Vilas enlisted him for three years in Madison, as a corporal in Company A, 23rd Wisconsin. He mustered in 25 August 1862 at Madison. He was married, age 26, and his home was Madison. He mustered out on 4 July 1865 at Mobile, Alabama. He was treated in the Regimental Hospital at New Iberia, Louisiana in November 1863 for wounds received from a gun shot in his right leg and left hand at Carrion Crow Bayou. He was shot in the hand between the thumb and index finger. He was in the Regimental Hospital at Mobile, Alabama in the spring of 1865, for fracture received on his right knee from an explosion there. According to the testimony of William Post, who was one of a detail of the company, diagonally across the street from the warehouse in which the ammunition surrendered by the rebels was being stored, in the city of Mobile, Alabama about 25 May 1865. He helped William Carey out of the rubbish and stated that he was severely bruised on the right knee and injured on his right ankle. William Post stated that he and Sergeant Carey were in his room at the time of the explosion and they both ran out into the street where shells were exploding in every direction. William Post helped him back into the building and left him on a chair while he went back to dig out the rest of the company who were buried in a fallen cotton gin. Until the following July he showed the effects of the injury to his right leg and was unfit for duty. At the time William

Carey was detailed issuing rations. After leaving the service he lived near Iowa City, Iowa from discharge until the spring of 1867 when he moved to Livingston County, Missouri where he was a farmer. He applied for an invalid pension on 19 December 1887.

His first wife, Leslie M. Jane, born 1844, died 1 November 1870. He married Emiline Rickett on 24 December 1871 at Livingston County, Missouri. She was born 24 February 1850 in Carroll County, Ohio, the daughter of John Rickett and Lydia Kelly. They had one child under the age of 16 in 1890, Joel was born 6 October 1890. He was living in Chillicothe, Missouri in 1889, but he did not attend the reunions of the 23rd Wisconsin Regiment in 1886 or 1889. In 1889, when William Carey was 52 years old, he was 5' 8 ½," weight 160 pounds. He was badly crippled in the right leg and in 1890 his pension was $2 per month. He died 14 May 1897 near Sturgus, Missouri and his widow, Emaline Carey filed for her widow pension on 17 June 1897.[87]

William Carey
(Signature of Claimant.)

---

[86] Wisconsin Adjutant General, Regimental Descriptive Rolls 1861-1865, 23rd Infantry, Company A. (FHL #1311689); National Archives, Washington D.C., Pension File: William Carey, Company A, 23rd Wisconsin Infantry, invalid pension filed 19 Dec 1887, application #632422, certificate #456964, filed in Missouri. Emaline Carey widow pension filed 17 Jun 1897, application #656439, certificate #462980, filed in Missouri; William H. Rickett of Spokane, Washington; Civil War Unit Histories, Part 4, The Union- Midwest and West: Regimental Histories and Personal Narratives. *The Survivors of the Twenty-third Regiment Wisconsin Volunteer Infantry*, 1889.

Dana, Napoleon Jackson Tecumseh   Major-General

He was born in Fort Sullivan, Eastport, Maine on 15 April 1822. He graduated in the United States military academy at West Point in 1842, and served on garrison duty until the Mexican war. They severely wounded him at the storming of Cerro Gordo, and he was made captain by brevet, for gallant conduct there. They promoted him captain on the staff and assistant quartermaster in 1848. He was on garrison duty, principally in Minnesota until 1855. He resigned to take up banking in St. Paul, serving there as brigadier-general of a state militia from 1857 to 1861. He raised and commanded the 1st Minnesota infantry in the first year of the war, and he was commissioned Brigadier-General in February 1862, attached to the Army of the Potomac. He served in the battles before Richmond, and commanded a brigade in General Sedgwick's division at Antietam. At that battle, he received such a serious wound that they carried him off the field for dead. In November 1862, he was commissioned Major-General of volunteers, and commanded the defenses of Philadelphia during Lee's invasion. Afterwards he joined the Army of the Gulf, and commanded an expedition by sea to the Rio Grande. They landed at Brazos Santiago, and drove the Confederate forces as far as Laredo. He successively commanded the 13th army corps, the district of Vicksburg, the 16th army corps, the districts of west Tennessee and Vicksburg, and the Department of the Mississippi. In May of 1865 he resigned from the army to pursue mining in the west. From 1866 to 1871, he was a general agent of the American-Russian commercial company of San Francisco, in Alaska and Washington. He became a superintendent of railroads in Illinois, and superintendent of the Chicago, Burlington & Quincy railroad in 1878. He was made chief of the old war and navy division, pension department in 1893. President Cleveland in 1895 promoted him first deputy commissioner of pensions. President McKinley removed him from the office in 1897.[88]

---

[87] *The Union Army* (Broadfoot Publishing Company; Wilmington, NC, 1998) vol. 8

Dennis, Elias Smith   Major General

He was born 4 December 1812 in Newburgh, New York. He was a resident of Carlyle, Illinois when the Civil War broke out. In August 1861 he became Lieutenant-Colonel of the 30th Illinois Infantry. When Colonel Philip B. Fouke resigned in April 1862, they promoted him Colonel. They promoted to Brigadier-General in November 1862 and in April 1865 promoted him to brevet Major-General of volunteers, for gallant and meritorious services in the operations before Mobile, Alabama. He died 17 December 1894. [89]

Elias Smith Dennis

---

[88] *The Union Army* (Broadfoot Publishing Company; Wilmington, NC, 1998) vol. 8:71

Dickey, Lieutenant

He was a Mexican, who was attached to the 1st Mexican cavalry or 2nd Texas Cavalry. They organized the regiment at Brownsville, Texas and the men were from Mexico.

Dickinson, Benjamin   Private - Company E, 23rd Wisconsin

He was born 9 March 1844 at Oneida County, New York. At an early age he was left an orphan and he moved before he was ten years old. On 9 August 1862, James M. Bull enlisted him for three years at Black Earth, as a private in Company E, 23rd Wisconsin. He mustered in 30 August 1862 at Madison. At the time of enlistment he was 5'5", single, 18, dark complexion, gray eyes, brown hair, and was a farmer in Black Earth. He mustered out on 4 July 1865 at Mobile, Alabama and applied for an invalid pension on 25 August 1887. He was living in Tama City, Iowa in 1889, but he did not attend the reunions of the 23rd Wisconsin Regiment in 1886 or 1889. After leaving the service he lived at Black Earth, Wisconsin; Conover, Cresco, Tama and Marshalltown, Iowa. In 1924 he was living in Marshalltown, Marshall County, Iowa. His occupation was farming, draying and mail service. He was a member of T. F. Bradford Post #24 of the G.A.R. Tama, Iowa. In July 1912, they recommended that he admit to the Iowa Soldiers' Home, as he was unable to support himself or family. In 1924 he asked for a pension increase due to high blood pressure, hardening of arteries, varicose veins, bad rupture, hemorrhoids, dizziness and heart trouble. Since 15 March 1923 *he needed aid and attendance of another person in dressing and undressing, at table, bathing, and going to the toilet. He wasn't confined to the house.*

He married Sophia C. Bergholz on 17 October 1870 at Brooklyn, Poweshiek County, Iowa. In 1915, their children were; Hattie E, born 4 April 1871, deceased; Albert B, born 3 January 1872, deceased; Sady M, born 17 November 1874 living in Fort Dodge, Iowa; Emma C, born 10 July 1877 living in Sioux City, Iowa; Arthur W, born 20 April 1880 living in Tama; Lula M, born 25 July 1885 living in Cedar Rapids, Iowa. In her widows' application, filed on 30 October 1931, Sophia Dickinson stated that during the first half of their marriage *he was more of less addicted to the liquor habit* and on an extended trip in Wisconsin, Grant and Lafayette counties, he *yielded to that habit to the limit and became for a time a confirmed inebriate* and left her at their home in Tama, Iowa without support. He frequently made trips thorough out Iowa pedaling spectacles. In the fall of 1899 he returned and made an *honest effort to control his pernicious alcoholic habit and gradually obtained full control of himself.* [90]

Benjamin Dickinson

---

[89] Wisconsin Adjutant General, Regimental Descriptive Rolls 1861-1865, 23rd Infantry, Company E. (FHL #1311689); National Archives, Washington D.C., Pension File: Benjamin Dickinson, Company E, 23rd Wisconsin Infantry, invalid pension filed: 25 August 1887, application #620460, certificate #413693 filed in Iowa. Sophia Dickinson widow pension filed: 30 Oct 1931, application #1705226, certificate #A-3-17-32 filed in Iowa. XC 2645392; Civil War Unit Histories, Part 4, The Union- Midwest and West: Regimental Histories and Personal Narratives. *The Survivors of the Twenty-third Regiment Wisconsin Volunteer Infantry*, 1889.

Duncan, John Elliott   Captain - Company B, 23rd Wisconsin

He was born about 1833 in Shippensburg, Pennsylvania, the son of John and Elizabeth Duncan. He learned the printer's trade at Carlisle, Pennsylvania, where he served a three-year apprenticeship. His first venture in the newspaper field was at Hemping, Illinois. He was publishing the *Republican* at Darlington, Wisconsin, which he owned at the outbreak of the Civil War, but he sold it before his entering the service. He enrolled for three years at Darlington, Wisconsin on 25 March 1862 and he mustered in on 29 August 1862, as a first lieutenant, age 29. He was promoted to Captain of Company B, 23rd Wisconsin Infantry on 20 February 1863. He was at the following battles: Chickasaw Bayou, Mississippi; Arkansas Post, Arkansas; Port Gibson, Mississippi; Champion Hills, Mississippi; Black River Bridge; Siege of Vicksburg, Mississippi; Carrion Crow Bayou, Louisiana; Sabine Cross Roads, Louisiana; Jackson, Louisiana. He mustered out at Mobile, Alabama on 4 July 1865 and he applied for an invalid pension on 2 June 1884. On 5 July 1863, while on the march from Vicksburg to Jackson, in Mississippi, he was overcome with heat and exhaustion, having symptoms of sunstroke. The next day they sent him back to Vicksburg to the company quarters, where Dr. O. H. Wood treated him. He was not in the hospital then or at any other time. He rejoined the company and shortly after received a leave of absence and returned home to Wisconsin for a short time. He suffered from the effects *of said exposure and injury on over-heating constantly up to the date of his discharge, and ever since. It has constantly affected him by pain in the head and eyes, vertigo and other similar symptoms.* Since his discharge he lived in Darlington, Wisconsin until 1871. There he was the publisher of *The Fayette County Union*. He then resided at or near Newton, Kansas where he was a farmer until 1877, when he went to Topeka, Kansas. There he was in a printing office for about two years. In 1879 he went to Eldora, Iowa where he remained, publishing a newspaper until the summer of 1882 when he removed to Ames, Iowa. In June of 1884 he was publishing the *Ames Intelligence*. Before his enrollment he was of sound physical health, free from pain in head and eyes, and vertigo. In 1884 he was disabled to the extent that he could not preform manual labor. In 1891 he applied for an increase of his invalid pension. He stated that *since receiving said sunstroke and from its effects that he has, at different time, been totally blind, each attack lasting different periods and increasing in severity.* He also stated that he has not been able for years to read plain print from Pica 7 without the aid of glasses. The sunstroke has also impaired his hearing, so much so *that hearing at times is difficult for him, conversation in the usual or common tone of voice.*

John E. Duncan married first Jennie Waugh in Hennepin, Illinois, who died 22 May 1862 at Darlington, Wisconsin. He had one child by his first wife, Fred A. Duncan, born in Florida, Illinois in April 1862. He married second Harriet Bray on 5 May 1869 by Reverend D. L. Leonard, at the home of her father at Darlington. She was born 19 June 1842 in Cornwall, near Plymouth, England, the daughter of William and Janey Bray Before her marriage, she was a teacher in Darlington. They had four children, three of whom died in infancy. Paul 1870-1870, Agnes 1874-1874 and Jessie 1877-1878. Ruth Duncan, born 11 January 1872 at Darlington, was the only one to survive. They moved to Ames in 1882 when they purchased the *Intelligencer*, which is 1915 was the *Tribune*, from John Watts. In the winter of 1885 E. W. Clark started a competing newspaper, which did not please Duncan. Clark was *young, inexperienced and ambitious and their feuding escalated in March 1886 when Clark charged Duncan with libel.* Duncan lost the case, and was awarded one dollar. They were living in Ames, Iowa in 1889 and he attended the 23rd Wisconsin's reunion in Madison on 15-16 September 1886. Mrs. Duncan was quite active in helping her husband with the paper until they sold it in 1890 to Henry Wilson. After selling the newspaper they appointed him the postmaster, which he held for four years. His health began to fail him and he died 6 October 1900 at Ames, of diabetes mellitus, complications of gangrenous ulcers, due to sunstroke followed by vertigo. The duration of the disease was twelve years, during which time he was practically an invalid. He was buried in Ames on 9 October 1900. His widow applied for her pension on 11 January 1901.In 1908 Harriet was living in Ames, Story County, Iowa. Harriet B. Duncan was admitted to the State Insane Hospital at Clarinda, Iowa in August 1914 and she died there 14 January 1915. She left no estate other than personal, which they turned over to her only heir, a daughter, Mrs. Ruth D. Tilden.[91]

---

[90] Wisconsin Adjutant General, Regimental Descriptive Rolls 1861-1865, 23rd Infantry, Company B. (FHL #1311689); National Archives, Washington D.C., Pension File: John E. Duncan, invalid pension filed: 2 Jun 1884, application #516122, certificate #306703, filed in Iowa. Harriet B. Duncan widow pension filed: 11 Jan 1901, application #732916, certificate #650987 in Iowa; Civil War Unit Histories, Part 4, The Union- Midwest and West: Regimental Histories and Personal Narratives. *The Survivors of the Twenty-third Regiment Wisconsin Volunteer Infantry*, 1889; Civil War Unit

124   Robert M. Addison: Civil War Diary

John Duncan
Farwell T. Brown Photographic Archive,
Ames Public Library 83.433.1-4

(Signature.)

Histories, Part 4, The Union- Midwest and West: Regimental Histories and Personal Narratives. *The Survivors of the Twenty-third Regiment Wisconsin Volunteer Infantry*, 1889; John E. Duncan obituary *The Intelligncer* 11 Oct 1900; Mrs. Harriet Bray Duncan obituaries *Ames Evening Times* 18 Jan 1915 & *Ames Weekly Tribune* 21 Jan 1915; *Story County, Iowa Grave Marker Inscriptions* p.647, Ames Muncipal Cemetery- Woodlawn, Section 3; Farwell T. Brown, *Ames the Early Years in Word and Picture From Marsh to Modern City*, 1993, p.60-62.

Ford, Cornelius   Private - Company E, 23rd Wisconsin

He was born 7 October 1833 in Fareham, Hampshire, England and before enlisting he lived in Indiana and Wisconsin. On 15 August 1862, James M. Bull enlisted him at Madison for three years, as a private in Company E, 23rd Wisconsin. He mustered in 30 August 1862 at Madison. He was married, age 28, 5'8", light complexion, grey eyes, brown hair, a farmer in Springfield, Dane, Wisconsin. He was captured at Carrion Crow Bayou, Louisiana on 3 November 1863 and he was listed in Parole camp New Orleans, Louisiana 27 December 1863, February and April 1864. He was also captured at Sabin Cross Roads, Louisiana on 8 April 1864. He mustered out with the company on 4 July 1865.

After leaving the service he moved from Springfield, Wisconsin to Charles City, Iowa in September 1866; to Chicago, Illinois April 1872; to Windsor, Florida in December 1905. He was living at 213 Campbell Avenue in Chicago in 1889 and he attended the 23rd Wisconsin's reunion in Madison on 15-16 September 1886. He applied for an invalid pension on 7 December 1891. In 1891 John W. Schreiner, grocer of Chicago, stated that Cornelius *has claimed to be unable to perform manual labor in the winter months on account of inability to endure cold weather. Due to defective nerve force caused by disease of the liver, indigestion and non assimilation of good. I know that he has gone to Florida for six winters, in part to escape the rigors of the winter months.* He also stated that in October 1890 he fell from a building (he was a carpenter) receiving injuries, which entirely disabled him for three months. He injured his back and two ribs were broken from the breast bone. Ever since then, he has been unfit for manual labor, except light duty. In 1891 they gave him a pension due to disease of the liver, indigestion, injury to spine, broken ribs and defective hearing. In 1907 his pension was $12 per month. In 1908 he was 5'3", weight 110 pounds, retired, mostly gray hair and his right arm was crooked having been broken at the elbow.

He married Ellen Hooker on 2 July 1855 at Prairie, she died 9 November 1909. His wife had to *take constant care of him as you would a child and she had no chance for any pleasure.* He died 20 May 1914, at his son's home (Clayton E. Ford) in Chicago, of nephritis cystitis and arteriosclerosis. He was buried in the Oak ridge Cemetery, near Chicago.[92]

Cornelius Ford
(Claimant's signature in full.)

---

[91] Wisconsin Adjutant General, Regimental Descriptive Rolls 1861-1865, 23rd Infantry, Company E. (FHL #1311689); National Archives, Washington D.C., Pension File: Cornelius Ford, Company E, 23rd Wisconsin Infantry, invalid pension filed: 7 Dec 1891, application #1076033, certificate #979812, filed in Illinois; Civil War Unit Histories, Part 4, The Union- Midwest and West: Regimental Histories and Personal Narratives. *The Survivors of the Twenty-third Regiment Wisconsin Volunteer Infantry,* 1889.

Frost, Louis D. First Lieutenant - Company I, 23rd Wisconsin

He was born 4 November 1841 in Troy, New York, the son of Richard Frost and Sarah M. Van Auden, both of New York. He had two sisters, Emma and Sarah and in 1850 and 1860 they were living in Blooming Grove, Dane county, Wisconsin. He was commissioned first Lieutenant on 11 May 1864 by the Governor of Wisconsin. He was single, aged 20, 5'7", medium complexion, blue eyes, brown hair, he was a farmer in Blooming, Dane County. He mustered in Company I, 23rd Wisconsin Infantry on 30 August 1862. A later record stated that he was a student at the University of Wisconsin. He was in the following actions: Chickasaw Bayou; Arkansas Post; Port Gibson; Champion Hills; Black River Bridge; Siege of Vicksburg; Jackson; Carrion Crow Bayou; Sabine Cross Roads. On 30 November 1863, they wounded him in the right hip with a minnie ball and he was taken a prisoner. They never extracted the minnie ball and they probed the wound about six inches downward and upward without finding the location of the ball. He was unable to run, walk fast and ascending a stairway was difficult for him. He mustered out on 4 July 1865. When he was 48 (1891), he received a pension of $4.00 per month. Five years later (1895) he was receiving $8.00 per month. After leaving the service he lived at Madison, Wisconsin; Winona, Minnesota; New York City; St. Cloud, Florida and Clearwater, Florida.

He married Julia Loretta Kar__ (?) in October 1872 in Madison, Wisconsin. He required the attention of his wife for some time before her death, then he lived with his daughter, Gertrude Frost Lucas in Clearwater, Florida. They had three children. Gertrude B, born 12 July 1873; Louis V, born 9 June 1877; Donald K, born 12 June 1883. He was living in Winona, Minnesota in 1889 and he attended the 23rd Wisconsin's reunion in Madison 15-16 September 1886. She died 2 February 1923 and was buried in St. Cloud, Florida. He died 15 August 1939 in St. Cloud, Florida. They allowed his daughter $100 for burial and funeral expenses. They listed the cause of death as paralysis of bowels, with the contributory cause listed as senility. His occupation, listed on his death certificate, was a certified accountant. [93]

---

[92] Wisconsin Adjutant General, Regimental Descriptive Rolls 1861-1865, 23rd Infantry, Company I. (FHL #1311689); National Archives, Washington D.C., Pension File: Louis D. Frost, Company I, 23 Wisconsin Infantry, invalid pension filed: 27 Apr 1878, application #253504, certificate #158275; Civil War Unit Histories, Part 4, The

Gill, Charles R.

He was born 17 August 1830 in Herkimer County, New York. He was a lawyer, politician and soldier. He studied law in Batavia, New York and was admitted to the bar. In 1854 he moved to Wisconsin, settling in Watertown where he was a police judge in 1857 and a city superintendent of schools from 1857 to 1859. A Democrat, he was state senator from 1860 to 1861. He was Colonel of the 29th Wisconsin Infantry, commissioned 20 August 1862 and mustered in 27 September 1862 at Madison. He was married, age 31, blue eyes, light brown hair, fair complexion, 5'6 1/2", a lawyer in Watertown. He resigned on 27 June 1863, due to ill health, and returned to his law practice in Watertown. With the outbreak of the war, he had become a Republican and in 1865 was elected state attorney general on that ticket. They reelected him in 1867 and served two terms from 1866 to 1870. In 1870 he moved to Blooming Grove and opened a law office in Madison. In 1876, President Grant appointed him commissioner of pensions, but he soon resigned and retired to his farm. He filed for an invalid pension on 11 September 1879. He alleged that at Port Gibson, Mississippi on 1 May 1863 *during the night after the battle, from his exertions, he was very sick prostrated, next morning was attacked with diarrhea and for several days had pain in his bones and back and suffered from insomnia, which continued until he went to the hospital on 17 June 1863.* After leaving the service the disability continued.

He married Martha A. Lancklon on 17 September 1854 at Wheatville, New York. They had the following children: Alice M., born 22 August 1868, Olive E. born 18 October 1870, Martha A., born 10 December 1875. He died 28 March 1883 and his widow, Martha A. Gill, filed for her widow pension on 27 April 1883.[94]

(Signature of Claimant.)

Union- Midwest and West: Regimental Histories and Personal Narratives. *The Survivors of the Twenty-third Regiment Wisconsin Volunteer Infantry*, 1889.
[93] Wisconsin Adjutant General, Regimental Descriptive Rolls 1861-1865, 29th Infantry, Field & Staff. (FHL #1311691); National Archives, Washington D.C., Pension File: Charles D. Gill, 29th Wisconsin, invalid pension filed: 11 Sep 1879, application #303918, certificate #163716. Martha A Gill widow pension filed: 27 Apr 1883, application #303687, certificate # 203173; *Dictionary of Wisconsin Biography* (The State Historical Society of Wisconsin: Madison, 1960) p. 143; E. B. Quiner, Esq.,

Greene, Joseph E. Captain - Company D, 23rd Wisconsin

On 20 August 1862, he enlisted as a Captain of Company D, 23rd Wisconsin Infantry, his home was Madison. He mustered in as major in Company E, 23rd Regiment, for three years at Iberia, Louisiana on 23 November 1863, married, age 31. Engagements: Chickasaw Bayou, Mississippi; Champion Hills; Arkansas Port, Arkansas; Port Gibson; Black River Bridge; Siege of Vicksburg; Siege of Jackson, Mississippi; Carrion Crow; Mansfield; Jackson, Louisiana; Siege of Spanish Fort; Blakely, Alabama. He mustered out with the company on 4 July 1865.[95]

Greene, William Corporal - Company C, 31st Wisconsin

He enlisted on 14 August 1862 as a corporal. He mustered into Company C, 31st Wisconsin Infantry, his home was Dodgeville. They listed him as a prisoner of war on 19 March 1865 in Bentonville, North Carolina and he mustered out on 22 June 1865.[96]

Guppy, Joshua James Colonel - 23rd Wisconsin

He was born 27 August 1820 in Dover, New Hampshire, the son of John Guppy and Hannah Dame or Dawe. He graduated at Portsmouth College in 1843, where in his senior year, he was Captain of the "Dartmouth Plalanx," the college military company. He studied law in Dover, New Hampshire and was admitted to the Bar in April 1844. In September of the next year, he settled in Columbus, Wisconsin, practicing his profession and doing a general land agency business. He remained there till 1851, when he moved to Portage where he had a beautiful homestead of fifty acres on Silver Lake. In February 1847, they appointed him Colonel of Militia and in September 1849, they appointed him Judge of Probate. He was elected County Judge six time, for terms of four years each, he was School Superintendent of the city of Portage. His elections to these offices were usually without opposition. In 1862 he was the Democratic candidate for Congress in the Second Wisconsin District, but was defeated by 2,000 votes, the

---

The Military History of Wisconsin. Chicago: Clarks & Co. Publishers, 1866. p. 1006-1007

[94] Wisconsin Adjutant General, Regimental Descriptive Rolls 1861-1865, 23rd Infantry, Company E. (FHL #1311689); Roster of Wisconsin Volunteers: War of the Rebellion

[95] Roster of Wisconsin Volunteers: War of the Rebellion

usual Republican majority being about 7,000. In 1868 he became a Republican, but he was never very active in politics. On 18 September 1861 he was commissioned Lieutenant Colonel of the 10th Regiment Wisconsin Volunteer Infantry. He served under General O. M. Mitchell in all his campaigns of 1861 and 1862 in Kentucky, Tennessee and Alabama. On 17 July 1862 he was promoted to Colonel of the 23d Regiment Wisconsin Volunteer Infantry. He was in command in the first assault at Vicksburg in December 1862, the capture of Post Arkansas, and at the battle of Grand Gulf, Port Gibson, Champion Hill, and Black River Bridge. Colonel Guppy was also in command of his regiment in the assault at Vicksburg in May 1863, and in the siege operations resulting in the capture of that stronghold, July 4, 1863. They transferred his regiment, with the 13th Army Corps to which it belonged, to the Department of the Gulf. At Carrion Crow they wounded him (just below the knee of the left leg), and subsequently taken a prisoner. The man who shot him was not thirty feet from him at the time. The Colonel commanded his men for some time after he was shot. Colonel Guppy was treated kindly while a prisoner and was exchanged in January 1864. In the summer of 1864 Colonel Guppy was assigned to the command of a brigade. He was in active service till the close of the war, all the way from Mobile Bay, Alabama to Paducah, Kentucky, and he was Port Commander at the latter place when the war ended. On 15 June 1865, Colonel Guppy was commissioned Brigadier General of Volunteers by brevet, *for gallant and meritorious service during the war*. His regiment was mustered out of service 4 July 1865, and had an enthusiastic reception on reaching Madison, Wisconsin, on July 16. On the 1 January 1866, he again entered upon his duties as County Judge, to which office he had been elected while serving in the army. In January 1882, at the close of his sixth term as County Judge, *due to impaired health from wounds, and from rheumatism contracted while in the army, General Guppey retired to private life, accepting business from a few of his old clients only.* He attended both reunions of the 23rd Regiment, the first at Madison 15-16 September 1886 and the second at Milwaukee, 28 August 1889. He was *never married, but notwithstanding that ill fortune, and his suffering from rheumatism, he retains his old time cheerfulness of spirit, and find much pleasure in the quiet days of his old age.* General Joshua J. Guppy was a member of Rousseau Post No. 14, G.A.R. He died 8 December 1893 in

Portage, Wisconsin.[97]

Harris, Gilbert Tyson   Private - Company E, 23rd Wisconsin

He was born 5 March 1846 in Mylon, in the Town of Kingston upon Hull. He was the only son of Solomon and Hannah Tyson Harris, who were married 3 January 1832 in Withern, Lincolnshire, England. On 4 January 1864 at Mazomanie, W. Brink enlisted him for three years, as a private in Company E, 23rd Wisconsin. He mustered in 9 January 1864 at Madison. He was 17, gray eyes, light hair, light complexion, 5'7", and they credited his enlistment to Mazomanie. Gilbert T. Harris died of acute dysentery in the General Hospital at Vicksburg, Mississippi on 6 November 1864, buried Section L, grave 130. His mother, Hannah Harris, filed for her mother pension on 14 March 1887. Gilbert had a sister, Emma Harris who was 11 years old when Gilbert enlisted and in 1864, his other sisters were Marian, age 26; Anna Maria, age 23; Hester, age 21; Alice, age 15. His father, Solomon could not provide for his family since 1853, because he was afflicted with double rupture and disease of his liver and bowels. Since the death of his son Gilbert, his afflictions grew worse. At the time of enlistment they rented a 40-acre farm near Dover, Wisconsin. They moved to the town of Helena, Iowa County, Wisconsin. They purchased the farm with bounty money from his son Gilbert T. Harris. They described the farm as being infertile, sandy and almost worthless. They estimated that it was worth $500, and it had a mortgage of $300.[98]

---

[96] Wisconsin Adjutant General, Regimental Descriptive Rolls 1861-1865, 23rd Infantry, Company E. (FHL #1311689); *Biographical Album of Wisconsin* (H. O. Brown & M. A. W. Mrown, 1888) v.2, p.752-754 (FHL #928508); Civil War Research and Genealogy Database (www.civilwardata.com) Historical Data Systems, Inc. P.O. Box 196, Kingston, MA 02364; International Genealogical Index version 4.01; Civil War Unit Histories, Part 4, The Union- Midwest and West: Regimental Histories and Personal Narratives. *The Survivors of the Twenty-third Regiment Wisconsin Volunteer Infantry*, 1889.

[97] National Archives, Washington D.C., Pension File: Gilbert T. Harris, Company E, 23rd Wisconsin Infantry, Hannah Harris mother pension filed 14 Mar 1887, application #351742, certificate #258456, filed in Wisconsin.

Horton, James Everett   Sergeant - Company E, 23rd Wisconsin

He was born 12 October 1845 at Chester, Geauga County, Ohio, the son of James Everett Horton and Susan M. Barker. On 14 August 1862 at Rutland, James M. Bull enlisted him for three years, as a sergeant in Company E, 23rd Wisconsin. He mustered in 30 August 1862 at Madison. He was single, age 18, his home was Rutland, Dane County. They appointed him Corporal on 12 February 1864, Sergeant 1 July 1864, reduced to ranks 21 March 1865 and he was reappointed Sergeant 1 May 1865. He mustered out with company on 4 July 1865 at Mobile, Alabama. He was first married to Minerva A. Prithard about 1868. His wife previously married Henry H. Morrell and they were divorced in Wisconsin May 1865. In 1915 both children, Forest and Jessie were dead. He was living in Minneapolis in 1889, but he did not attend the reunions of the 23rd Wisconsin Regiment in 1886 or 1889. In 1905 he was a farmer, height 5'4", weight 118; grey eyes, light hair and complexion. After leaving the service he lived in Wisconsin, then Minneapolis til 1905. He filed for an invalid pension on 21 October 1907 and he died 22 October 1919 at Princeton, Minnesota.[99]

---

[98] Wisconsin Adjutant General, Regimental Descriptive Roll 1861-1865, 23rd Infantry, Company E. (FHL #1311689); National Archives, Washington D.C., Pension File: James E. Horton, Company E, 23rd Wisconsin Infantry, invalid pension filed: 21 Oct 1907, application #1367865, certificate #1141170, filed in MN, C2480186; Ancestral File, version n419 submitted 1996, 1997; Civil War Unit Histories, Part 4, The Union- Midwest and West: Regimental Histories and Personal Narratives. *The Survivors of the Twenty-third Regiment Wisconsin Volunteer Infantry*, 1889; Organization index to pension files of veterans FHL #1726106.

Jolley, John Lawlor
Second Lieutenant -Company C, 23rd Wisconsin

He was born 14 July 1840 at Montreal, Province of Quebec, the son of James and Frances Lawlor Jolley, who had come from Ireland about 1838. In 1846, when he was six years old, his parents moved to the city of Hamilton, Ontario and there he attended a private school. In 1853 his father began teaching him the trade of harness making. On 1 May 1857 he moved to Portage City where he began the study of law in the following year. He was admitted to the bar of the state in October 1861. He mustered in as a private on 30 August 1862 at Madison, single, aged 22, his home was Portage, Columbia County. At the time of enlistment he was a law student, 5'6", weight 140, hazel eyes, brown hair, dark complexion and he had a scar about four inches long on his right side. On 21 July 1863, the Governor of Wisconsin, commissioned him, for three years, as second lieutenant in Company C, 23rd Wisconsin. He saw action at Chickasaw Bayou; Arkansas Post; Port Gibson; Champion Hills; Black River Bridge; Siege of Vicksburg; Jackson; Carrison Crow Bayou. He mustered out on 4 July 1865. After they discharged him, he lived at Portage City, Wisconsin. He went to school in Chicago, Illinois from February to May 1866 where he took a short course of study in the Eastman Commercial College. On 10 July 1866 he went to the territory of Dakota, where he became one of the pioneers of the city of Vermillion, Clay county. He took up a homestead north of town and made improvements while he established his law practice. He went on to become one of the oldest practitioners in that section of the state. He was a stalwart advocate of the principals of the Republican party and was a prominent figure, wielding much influence. He was elected a member of the Dakota house of representatives in 1867, and reelected in 1868. He was a member of the Dakota territorial counsel in 1875 and 188, elected state senator in 1889, and reelected in 1890. He was mayor of Vermilion in 1877 and 1885; delegate to the Republican National Convention in 1884; a member of the constitutional convention in 1889; a member of the State senate in 1889 and 1890; elected as a Republican to the Fifty-second Congress to fill the vacancy caused by the death of John R. Gamble and served from 7 December 1891, to 3 March 1893. He was not a candidate for renomination. In the *Capital Journal* dated January 1891, the following appeared: *Jolley of Clay County is said to be Jolly just like his name. The wit seems to flow as freely as it did last winter*. He resumed his law practice. They always recognized him as a citizen of utmost loyalty and highest public spirit. He was especially interested in the state university and assisted in getting the location in Vermillion. His efforts and enthusiasm also helped raise the money needed to replace the building when fire destroyed it. He was a member of the Miner Post, No. 8, Grand Army of the Republic.

Harriet J. Grange was born 5 March 1851 at Dubuque, Iowa. She married John L. Jolley on 20 April 1874 at Dubuque. They had the following children: Frances D. Jolley, born 18 January 1875, who married the Honorable Charles H. Dillon, a member of the bar of Yankton; Charles W. born 31 May 1878, a successful farmer of Clay County; Mary L. born 31 May 1878. The Jolley School was named for John L. Jolley, pioneer lawyer, who taught school in the old log schoolhouse during the winter of 1866-1867. The original site of the house was below the bluff and the house somehow survived the flood of 1881 and was then moved to 22 High Street in Vermillion. They sold the house in 1971 and was later torn down. In 1902, the Jolley Elementary (East Side) School was built on South University Street, in Vermillion. He died 14 December 1926 at Vermillion, buried in Bluff View Cemetery. By proclamation of the Mayor Viers, all business houses in Vermillion were closed from 9:45 to 11:00, as a tribute of respect to the memory of Mr. Jolley on the day of the funeral. The Center for Western Studies at Augustana College in Sioux Falls, South Dakota has a collection of his papers and correspondence, 1871 to 1921. The material includes correspondence, legal documents, printed materials and photos relating to his life and career. [100]

---

[99] Wisconsin Adjutant General, Regimental Descriptive Rolls 1861-1865, 23rd Infantry, Company C. (FHL #1311689); National Archives, Washington D.C., Pension File: John L. Jolley, Company C, 23rd Wisconsin Infantry, invalid pension filed: 22 May 1902, application #1403617, certificate #1170511 from South Dakota. Harriet Jolley widow pension filed: 28 Apr 1927, application #1578622, certificate #A7-19-27 from South Dakota; Doane Robinson, *History of South Dakota* (B. F. Bowen & Co., 1904) vol.2, page 1371; Herringshaw's *Encyclopedia of American Biography* page 536; *Biographical Directory of the United State Congress; Clay County Place Names*, 1976, p.78, 136; *Biographical Directory of the South Dakota Legislature 1889-1989*, vol.1, p.561; John L. Jolley obituary, Vermillion, South Dakota, 16 December 1926; Donarae Albers Jolley of Blunt, South Dakota.

John L. Jolley

Jones, John G. Corporal - Company G, 23rd Wisconsin

On 21 August 1862 at Columbus, J. T. Hazelton enlisted him for three years, as a corporal in Company G, 23rd Wisconsin. He mustered in 30 August 1862 at Madison, He was single, age 19 and his home was Columbus, Columbia County. They killed him in action on 5 October 1864 at Jackson, Louisiana, near Sandy Bayou, Louisiana.[101]

---

[100] Wisconsin Adjutant General, Regimental Descriptive Rolls 1861-1865, 23rd Infantry, Company G. (FHL #1311689)

Jussen, Carl   Adjutant - Company E, 23rd Wisconsin

He was born 29 January 1843 at Julich, Prussia, the son of Jacob and Catharine Auertz Jussen. On 24 November 1863, he enlisted for three years as an adjutant in Company E, 23rd Wisconsin. He mustered in 2 August 1863 at Algier's, Louisiana. His engagements were Chickasaw Bayou, Mississippi; Arkansas Post, Arkansas; Port Gibson; Champion Hills; Black River Bridge; Siege of Vicksburg; Siege of Jackson, Mississippi: Carrion Crow Bayou; Sabine Cross Roads, Louisiana.

He married Camilla J. Shaler on 14 October 1868 in New York City. She was the daughter of Alexander Shaler and Margaret Murray. He filed for an invalid pension, connected to Company D, 23 Wisconsin Infantry, on 26 July 1904. He was a clerk both prior and after the war. After leaving the service he resided in Watertown, Wisconsin; New York City; Ridgefield, Fairview and Newark, New Jersey. They had the following children; Katrina Ruetz, born 31 December 1869; Alexander Shaler born 18 April 1875; Carl born 1 April 1878, died 1 June 1878; Frederic Carl born 18 July 1879; Mary Louise born 10 October 1881. In 1904 he was 61 years old, 5'9", 135 pounds, fair complexion, blue eyes, gray hair, a clerk. He died on 8 March 1919 at New York City, New York. His widow, Camilla J. Jussen died at her home 10 Brookfield Road, Upper Montelair, New Jersey on 4 January 1933. His widow filed for her pension on 10 April 1919 and she received $40 a month.[102]

---

[101] Wisconsin Adjutant General, Regimental Descriptive Rolls 1861-1865, 23rd Infantry, Company E. (FHL #1311689); National Archives, Washington D.C., Pension File: Carl Jussen, Company D, 23rd Wisconsin Infantry, invalid pension filed: 26 Jul 1904, application #1321401, certificate #1095838 from New Jersey. Camille J. Jussen widow pension filed: 10 Apr 1919, application #1139290, certificate #868677 from New York; Organization index to pension files of veterans, Adjt F&S 23rd, FHL #1726106.

Kinsey, William Baker   Brigadier- General

He was born 11 May 1836 in Willistown, Chester County, Pennsylvania, the son of Dr. John and Margaret Woodward Kinsey. He mustered in as private in Company A, 23rd New York Infantry, in September 1862 as a first-lieutenant, 161st New York Infantry. He was a lieutenant-colonel in July 1863, then brevet brigadier-general in March 1865. He commanded the 3rd brigade, division 1, 13th Corps of the Army and Department of the Gulf from March through April 1865.

He married Ada Lelia Wenzell, on 29 January 1868 at Philadelphia, a Friends Ceremony. The record is filed with the Green Street Monthly Meeting. She was born 6 March 1847 in Pennsylvania, the daughter of Samuel S. Wenzell and Laura M. Salter. Ada died 8 April 1935 in Philadelphia. They had three children; Virginia Elmira (married Joseph John Farland) born 19 Jan 1870, Alice Louise (married Nelson F. Eberback) born 16 Jun 1872, Helen Fairchild Kinsey born 12 August 1877. He was a member of Post No. 2 G. A. R.; Pennsylvania Commanandery and Military Order of the Loyal Legion. In 1902 he was 5' 4 ½", 130 pounds, hazel eyes, grey hair, light complexion. His pension in 1906 was $12 per month, due to total inability to earn a support by manual labor. He died 21 January 1919 in Philadelphia, Pennsylvania of cerebral effrision, and was cremated.[103]

William B Kinsey
(Signature.)

---

[102] Civil War Research and Genealogy Database (www.civilwardata.com) Historical Data Systems, Inc. P.O. Box 196, Kingston, MA 02364; Obituary *Philadelphia Public Ledger*, 23 January 1919; National Archives, Washington D.C., Pension File:William B. Kinsey, brig general, 161 , A 23 NY Infantry, , invalid pension filed: 17 Oct 1902, application #1291911, certificate #1055921 from Pennsylvania. Widow pension filed: 27 Jan 1919, application #1134954, certificate #867292 from Pennsylvania.

Landram, William Jennings   Brevet Brigadier-General

He was born 11 February 1828 in Lancaster, Kentucky, the eldest son of Lewis and Martha George Landram. His father was a lawyer from Virginia and William received a liberal education in the best private schools. In 1845 he became deputy clerk for the county and circuit courts of Garrard County. During the Mexican war he enlisted as a private in Company A of the First Kentucky Cavalry. At the end of the first month they promoted him to orderly sergeant. They wounded him at the battle of Buena Vista. At the end of his enlistment he returned to his place in the clerk's office, reading law during his leisure moments. In 1850 and 1851 he edited and published the *Garrard Banner*, a political journal. In 1854 he was elected clerk of the circuit court of Garrard County, and was continually reelected and held the office until the being of the civil war. In 1861 he entered the Government service at Camp Rick Robinson and was commissioned colonel of the First Kentucky Cavalry. He resigned from that position, as he did not like cavalry service. Under orders from General Sherman he took charge of the Government grounds at Harrodsburg and in two months recruited the Nineteenth Kentucky Infantry Regiment. They promoted him to Colonel January 1862 of 19th Kentucky Infantry, then brevet brigadier-general in March 1865. Commanded brigades 1 & 2 in 4th division, 13th Corps of the Army and Department of the Gulf. At the end of the war he returned to his home in Lancaster. President Johnson appointed him a collector of internal revenue for the Eighth Kentucky District, and held the position by successive appointments until July 1885. Then he entered a law practice at Lancaster.

In 1848 he married Sarah Walker, a daughter of William Walker of Bath County. They had nine children, and six were living in 1887; Walker, Mary (married Mr. Burnside), Addie (married Mr. McFarland), Ella (married Mr. Dunlap), Lewis and Katie. The General and Mrs. Landram were members of the Presbyterian Church. He was a Mason and an I.O.O.F. and he died 11 October 1895 in Lancaster, Kentucky. Sarah was awarded a pension of $30 per month in 1898. [104]

---

[103] Civil War Research and Genealogy Database (www.civilwardata.com) Historical Data Systems, Inc. P.O. Box 196, Kingston, MA 02364; W. H. Perrin. *Kentucky. A History of the State* . . .F. A. Battey and Company, 1887. pp. 174-175; National Archives, Washington D.C., Pension File:William B. Kinsey, brig general, 161 , A 23 NY Infantry, , invalid pension filed: 15 Aug 1890, application #795990,, certificate

Lull, Frank H. Second Lieutenant - Company G, 23rd Wisconsin

He was born 13 March 1836 in London, Canada, the son of Henry Lull and Caroline Russell. Before he entered the service in August 1861, he was living in Columbus, Wisconsin where he was a farmer. He entered as a private in the 7th Wisconsin Volunteer Infantry. They transferred him to the 23rd Wisconsin September 1862, and joined the Regiment at Covington, Kentucky on 18 September 1862. On 18 June 1863, the Governor of Wisconsin commissioned him, for three years, as a first lieutenant. At the time of his enlistment he was married, 26, gray eyes, black hair, fair complexion, 5'10", a farmer in Ripon, Fond du Lac County. They promoted him to 2nd lieutenant in the 23rd Wisconsin, Company G on 19 March 1863. He was the only officer present with the Company through the actions of Port Gibson, Champion Hills, Black River Bridge and the siege of Vicksburg. He was wounded him twice, but he was never in the hospital. He was relieved from duty at Galveston, Texas on 8 August 1865, and ordered to report to Colonel Sheldon Sturgeon, Chief Mustering Officer, Department of Louisiana and Texas. He received orders to report to Alexandria for temporary duty but was he was taken ill and not able to comply with orders immediately. On 21 August 1865 he learned that his mother was very sick and requested a leave of absence or discharge.

After leaving the service he lived at Eagle, Missouri from October 1865 until March 1866; then March 1866 to November 1892 at Plano, Illinois; then November 1892 until May 1902 at Chicago. In 1902 he was 5' 7" and weighed 130 pounds, grey eyes and hair, fair complexion. He married Laura Jane Kendall on Thanksgiving Day 1860 at Chicago, but the record of the marriage was lost in the Chicago Fire in 1871. They had six children, five of whom were alive in 1914. Effie, born 31 January 1862; Albert born 17 May 1866; Harry, born 21 April 1870; Frank born 23 August 1871; and Lyle born 27 February 1873. Frank Lull died on 23 March 1914 at the Wisconsin Veteran Home in Farmington of Angina pectoris. [105]

---

cert #550226 from Kentucky. Sarah A. Landram, Widow pension filed: 17 Apr 1898 application #675406, certificate #464062.

[104] Wisconsin Adjutant General, Regimental Descriptive Rolls 1861-1865, 23rd Infantry, Company G. (FHL #1311689); Service Records, National Archives, Washington, D.C.; National Archives, Washington D.C., Pension, Frank H Lull, Company G, 23rd Wisconsin Infantry, invalid pension filed: 14 Jun 1902, application ##1286326, certificate #1055812 from Wisconsin. Widow pension filed: 27 Mar 1914,

Frank G. Bull
(Signature.)

Marsh, Francis G. Lieutenant - Company B, 23rd Wisconsin

He was born 12 January 1823 at Windham, Vermont. When he was 21 years of age he enlisted in Company 1, 2d U. S. regular infantry and served in the Mexican war as a sergeant. He was a first lieutenant, in Company B, 23rd Wisconsin Regiment. He was commissioned 31 October 1863, for three years. He mustered in as sergeant on 29 August 1862 at Madison. He was married, age 39, 5' 7 ½," hazel eyes, black hair, a clothier. He saw action; Chickasaw Bayou, Mississippi; Arkansas Post, Arkansas; Port Gibson, Mississippi; Champion Hills, Mississippi; Black River Bridge, Mississippi; Siege of Vicksburg, Mississippi; investment of Jackson, Mississippi; Carrion Crow Bayou, Louisiana; Jackson, Louisiana; Fort Spanish and Balkely, Alabama. In 1885 he was living in Darlington, Wisconsin. He was living in Darlington, Wisconsin in 1889. He attended both reunions of the 23rd Wisconsin, the first at Madison 15-16 September 1886 and the second at Milwaukee, 28 August 1889.

He married Mary A. Kellum on 5 July 1850 in Dodge County, Wisconsin and she died at Darlington on 2 March 1898. In 1893 he was living in Darlington. The only real estate he owned was a lot in the City of Darlington, eight rods square with a small house, not worth more than eight hundred dollars. He raised a few bushels of potatoes and other vegetables on the lot for his own consumption. His personal property was a cow and a note of eight hundred dollars against Mrs. H. B. White of Darlington, which drew 8% interest. He had $200 in the bank, but needed to pay his medical bills with it in 1897. He then moved to Windom in 1900. He had three sons, Carlos E. Marsh born 2 May 1851, Freeman L. Marsh born 19 March 1857 and Reuben F. Marsh born 2 October 1864. In Windom they knew him as the only Mexican war veteran in the area. He was 92 years old and had enjoyed

application #1024805, certificate #774892, from Illinois.

comparatively good health until he fell and fractured his hip, about two weeks before he died. He died at the home of his son, on 25 October 1914 at Windom, Minnesota and was buried next to his wife in Darlington.[106]

Francis G. Marsh

---

[105] Wisconsin Adjutant General, Regimental Descriptive Rolls 1861-1865, 23rd Infantry, Company B. (FHL #1311689); Tabular statements of the census enumeration and the agricultural, mineral and manufacturing interests of the State of Wisconsin also alphabetical list of the soldiers and sailors of the late war residing in the state June 20, 1885. (Wisconsin, Wis: Democrat Printing Company, State Printers, 1886.) FHL # 977.5 X2w, p. 215 Marsh, F. G. 1ST Lieutenant regt co. B state- Wisconsin post office Darlington; Civil War Unit Histories, Part 4, The Union- Midwest and West: Regimental Histories and Personal Narratives. *The Survivors of the Twenty-third Regiment Wisconsin Volunteer Infantry*, 1889; Organization index to pension files of veterans FHL #1726106, Francis G. Marsh, also served Mexican War C, 3. 148, Co B, 23rd, invalid filed 7 Jun 1892 & 18 Feb 1907, app#1083636, cert #1000391; Obituary *Citizen* 4 October 1914.

McClellan, George Brinton   Major General

He was born 3 December 1826 in Philadelphia, Pennsylvania, the son of George McClellan and Elizabeth Steinmetz Brinton. He was a major-general who attended the University of Pennsylvania in 1841, where he stayed for nearly two years. In 1842 he entered the U. S. military academy and he graduated second in the class of 1846. He was first in the class in engineering. In June 1846 he was commissioned brevet second lieutenant of engineers. He married Mary Ellen Marcy. In May 1861 they promoted him to major-general. In 1861 he commanded the Army of Occupation West Virginia and August 1861 to November 1862 commanded the Army of Potomac. He died 29 October 1885 in Orange, New Jersey.[107]

George Brinton McClellan

---

[106] *The Union Army* (Broadfoot Publishing Company; Wilmington, NC, 1998) vol. 8:162-165; Ancestral File version n419, submitted in 1995.

McCormack, Charles

He was born 1 January 1840 in Rush County, Indiana and moved near Madison, Wisconsin in 1845. He studied medicine one year at Madison. At the out break of the Civil War he enlisted in the 2nd Wisconsin Cavalry and served two years. Due to illness they discharged him and afterward he reenlisted in the 35th Wisconsin Infantry where he served two years as First Lieutenant. On 10 February 1864, the Governor of Wisconsin commissioned him for three years, in Company D, 35th Regiment. At the time of enlistment he was 22 years, height 5'10 ½," dark complexion, dark hair, dark eyes, a farmer of Sun Prairie. He mustered in 18 February 1864. After leaving the army he resumed his study of medicine, graduating in 1867. He filed for an invalid pension on 6 May 1886. He contracted typhoid fever that resulted in heart disease, rheumatism and disease of the lower limbs. They treated him at Helena, Arkansas during the fall of 1863.

He married Jennette Jones on 25 July 1867 at Charles City, Iowa. They had the following children: Carroll, born 27 July 1882 and Howard born 18 June 1885. Since leaving the service he lived in Iowa and Kansas and his occupation had been a student and physician. Dr. Alleyne sold out to Dr. McCormick. They described him *as a well-informed man and a good physician, but some of his practice was along lines of not a high character*. In 1886 he was living in Waverly, Iowa, age 46, weight 185 pounds. He died 4 May 1897 at Algona, Iowa of mitral disease of the heart, buried May 6 at Algona. He had been arranging to leave Algona and had shipped his goods to Wesley and Mrs. McCormack was on a visit with her daughter when called home to attend him. He was a member of the Masonic order, which had charge of the funeral. He died at his room over the Hulbert restaurant. His health had been failing rapidly and he had been troubled for many years with an abdominal tumor. He had consulted many doctors about it, but was not willing to risk a surgical operation for its removal. The year before his death he requested that a local physician hold a post mortem examination if he died in Algona. The doctors found that his trouble originally was a ventral hernia through which a fold of the covering of the intestines protruded. This covering gradually hardened into a sort of fatty tumor to which a fold of the intestine was adherent. The adhesions formed an intestinal obstruction that gave the doctor great trouble just before his death. They also showed it at the post mortem, as different physicians had told him, that he suffered from gall stones. A dozen or more gall stones were found varying in size from a large hazel nut to a small pea. The immediate cause of death was probably intestinal obstruction. His widow, Jennette McCormack, filed her widow pension on 28 June 1897.[108]

[Signature of Claimant]

McGinnis, George Francis   Brigadier-General

He was born 19 March 1826 in Boston, Massachusetts, reared by an aunt in Maine and moved with his father to Chillocothe, Ohio. He enlisted in the Mexican War as a lieutenant in the 2nd Ohio Volunteers and was mustered out in 1848 as a captain. In 1850 he moved to Indianapolis and began manufacturing hats. When Fort Sumter surrendered on 14 April 1861, he joined the three-month 11th Indiana Volunteer Infantry as a private. He was commissioned a captain on April 16, and the Lieutenant Colonel on April 25, on 6 September 1861 he became Colonel of the regiment. They assigned the 11th, under the command of Lew Wallace, to duty in Cumberland, Maryland, and was successful in chasing the Confederates from Romney, (West) Virginia, in June. Having completed their enlistment, they mustered them out in Indianapolis on August 2. They then reorganized the 11th as a three-year unit and in September they appointed him the commanding colonel. The 11th spent the early winter of 1861- 62 at Paducah, Kentucky, and in February participated in Ulysses S. Grant's victories at Forts Henry and Donelson, Tennessee. At Shiloh, Tennessee, McGinnis made the march with Wallace on the first day and was in temporary command of a brigade. In December 1862, they assigned him to permanent brigade command in the District of Eastern

---

[107] Wisconsin Adjutant General, Regimental Descriptive Rolls 1861-1865, 35th Infantry, Company D. (FHL #1311693); National Archives, Washington D.C., Pension File: Charles McCormack, Company F, 2nd Wisconsin Cavalry & Company D, 35 Wisconsin Infantry and Quarter Master, 2nd Wisconsin Cavalry, invalid pension filed: 6 May 1886, application #572625, certificate # 494991. Jennette McCormack, widow pension filed: 28 Jun 1897, application #657288 certificate #456145; Obituary *Algona Upper Des Moines*, 5 May 1897 and *The Algona Courier*, 7 May 1897; Benjamin F. Reed *History of Kossuth County*, 1913, p.618.

Arkansas. He participated in the Yazoo Pass, Mississippi, operation in February and was made a brigadier general in April ranking from the previous November. He was active in the Vicksburg Campaign in May-June-July. For the balance of the War, they gave McGinnis minor assignments, such as cavalry companies and infantry regiments in the Department of the Gulf, Military Division of West Mississippi, Reserve Corps and U.S. Forces Mouth of White River. After the War he was not breveted a major general, the routine honor for most brigadier generals. Returning to Indianapolis he became the county auditor, 1867-71. They appointed him to various public offices and in 1900 was the postmaster of Indianapolis. He died in Indianapolis on 29 May 1910 and was cremated, they buried his ashes at Crown Hill Cemetery. [109]

Mohr, Oscar   Captain - Company G, 29th Wisconsin
He enlisted on 2 September 1862 as first lieutenant, and his home was Cross Plains Wisconsin. He was commissioned a captain in Company G, 29th Wisconsin Infantry. He mustered out on 22 June 1865 at Shreveport, Louisiana. He filed for an invalid pension on 15 April 1908. His widow, filed for her widow pension on 4 December 1908. His pension file has been lost or destroyed, according to the Department of Veteran Affairs. [110]

North, David   Private - Company D, 23rd Wisconsin
He enlisted on 14 August 1862 as a private in company D, 23rd Wisconsin Infantry, his home was Madison. He mustered in on the same day. He died of disease on 19 March 1863 at Milliken's Bend, Louisiana.[111]

---

[108] *The Union Army* (Broadfoot Publishing Company; Wilmington, NC, 1998) vol. 8:42; Indiana in the Civil War, http://www.thnet.com/~liggetkw/incw/hoosier/mcginnis.htm
[109] General Index to Pension Files 1861-1934 (FHL #0541087); Roster of Wisconsin Volunteers: War of the Rebellion; National Archives, Washington D.C., Pension File: Oscar Mohr, Company G, 29th Wisconsin Infantry, invalid pension filed: 15 Apr 1908, application #1373127, certificate #1147850, filed from Wisconsin. Emilie Mohr widow pension filed: 4 Dec 1908, application #908990, certificate #672508, filed from Wisconsin. XC2680 417.
[110] The diary mentions a Captain North of the 29th Wisconsin, but there wasn't one in that regiment; Roster of Wisconsin Volunteers: War of the Rebellion

Norton, John G.   Lieutenant - Company I, 23rd Wisconsin
He mustered in as sergeant, Company I, 23rd Wisconsin Infantry, 30 May 1862 at Madison, single, age 24, home was Madison, Dane County. The Governor of Wisconsin commissioned him, 2nd lieutenant on 18 June 1863 for three years. Actions: Chickasaw Bayou; Arkansas Post; Port Gibson; Champion Hill; Black River Bridge; Siege of Vicksburg; Jackson; Carrion Crow Bayou; Sabine Cross Roads.

He applied for an invalid pension filed on 1 March 1879. In 1890, when he was 41, he was 5'7", 145 pounds, light complexion. He married Olivia C. Buchner on 18 February 1886 at Monroe County, Wisconsin. He died 30 September 1891 and his widow, Olivia C. Norton, filed for her widow pension 27 June 1892. In 1902 she had 105 acres of rough stony land, half woods assessed at $200. A house (built 30 years ago) and lot worth $400, personal property, including live stock and goods in store $457. She kept a small store with a stock of good worth between $300 and $400 for which she still owed. She had a hired man to look after the stock, but after paying him she did not net income. His widow, Olivia C. Norton died at the Chippewa County asylum on 18 July 1911.[112]

---

[111] Wisconsin Adjutant General, Regimental Descriptive Rolls 1861-1865, 23rd Infantry, Company I. (FHL #1311689); National Archives, Washington D.C., Pension File: John G. Norton, Company I, 23rd Wisconsin Infantry, invalid pension filed on 1 Mar 1879, application #270019, certificate #171423. Olivia C. Norton widow pension filed: 27 Jun 1892, application #553735, certificate #549648, filed in Wisconsin.

Ord, Edward Otho Cresap   Brigadier-General

He was born in Cumberland, Maryland, on 18 October 1818, the third son of James and Rebecca Ruth (Cresap) Ord. His father was a United States naval officer, and his mother was the daughter of Daniel Cresap, an officer in the American Revolution. The family moved to Washington, D.C., when he was a year old and that is where he received his early schooling. They appointed him to the United States Military Academy at West Point in September 1835 at the age of sixteen. After graduating seventeenth in the class of 1839, they commissioned him as a second lieutenant in the Third Artillery Regiment. After field service against the Florida Seminoles, they promoted him to first lieutenant two years later. During the Mexican War they stationed him in California and in 1850 they promoted him to captain on Indian duty in the Pacific Northwest. He participated in the suppression of the John Brown insurrection at Harpers Ferry in 1859. At the time of the firing on Fort Sumter, he was back in California, stationed at the Presidio. He received a commission as brigadier general of volunteers on 14 September 1861. During the first year of the Civil War he commanded a brigade assigned to defend the capital. He participated in a skirmish with Jeb Stuart's cavalry at Dranesville, Virginia, on 20 December 1861 and was promoted to major general of volunteers on 2 May 1862 and was transferred to the western theater of operations. At the battle of Iuka, Mississippi, on 19 September 1862, they gave him a colonel's brevet in the regular army *for gallant and meritorious service* on the field, but he was not near the battlefield. They severely wounded him a few days later at Hatchie, Mississippi, and he did not return until June 1863, when he took part in the siege of Vicksburg as commander of the Thirteenth Corps. After the fall of Vicksburg on July 4, He held commands in Louisiana and in the Shenandoah Valley of Virginia. During the siege of Richmond he commanded first the Eighth Corps and later the Eighteenth Corps. They seriously wounded him at the storming of Fort Harrison in September 1864 and did not return to his command until January 1865. On 13 March 1865, they awarded him the brevet rank of brigadier general for his role in the battle of Hatchie, Mississippi. He received a major general's brevet for his part in the assault on Fort Harrison, Virginia. They then gave him command of the Army of the James with responsibility for the Department of North Carolina. He became a brigadier general in the regular United States Army on 26 July 1866.

After the surrender of the Confederate armies, he commanded the Fourth Military District and then the military departments of California and the Platte before receiving assignment to command the Military Department of Texas on 11 April 1875. He supervised the construction of Fort Sam Houston, where his command numbered from 3,000 to 3,900 troops, stationed at San Antonio and forts Brown, Concho, Clark, Davis, Duncan, McKavett, and Ringgold. From his headquarters at San Antonio Ord oversaw the scouting, construction of telegraph lines, and post maintenance and repair, and suppression of cattle rustling and hostile Indians. Troops under his command were responsible for the discovery of grazing land in the state's trans-Pecos region and deposits of silver, iron, lead, and copper.

He married Mary Mercer Thompson at San Francisco on 14 October 1854. They had two sons and a daughter. He retired from active duty on 6 December 1880, with the rank of major general. He was stricken with yellow fever on a cruise ship bound from New York to Veracruz and died in Havana on July 22, 1883. They buried him at Arlington National Cemetery. [113]

---

[112] *The Union Army* (Broadfoot Publishing Company; Wilmington, NC, 1998) vol. 8; The Handbook of Texas Online, Http://www.tsha.utexas.edu/handbook/online/articles/view/OO/for1.html, *Thomas W. Cutrer* - Robert W. Callaway, General Edward Otho Cresap Ord, Commander of the Military Department of Texas, 1874-1880 (M.A. thesis, University of Texas, 1954). *Dictionary of American Biography*. Francis B. Heitman, *Historical Register and Dictionary of the United States Army* (2 vols., Washington: GPO, 1903; rpt., Urbana: University of Illinois Press, 1965). Vertical Files, Barker Texas History Center, University of Texas at Austin. Ezra J. Warner, *Generals in Blue* (Baton Rouge: Louisiana State University Press, 1964).

Parkin, Benjamin   Private - Company E, 23rd Wisconsin

He was born about 1840 in England. On 8 September 1862 at Madison, T. S. West enlisted him for three years, as a private, Company A, 11th Wisconsin. He was married, blue eyes, brown hair, fair complexion, 5'11". He mustered in on 8 September 1862 at Madison. Engaged in these battles: Champion Hills, Mississippi; Big Black River Bridge, Mississippi; Siege of Vicksburg, Mississippi and the assault on the works; Siege of Jackson, Mississippi. He transferred to Company E, 23rd Wisconsin Volunteers 10 February 1864. Engaged in: Sabine Cross Roads, Louisiana and mustered out on 31 May 1865. [114]

He applied for an invalid pension on 5 May 1882. While on picket duty at Brashear City, Louisiana on 8 January 1864 he contacted rheumatism. He was on duty twenty-four hours straight, and when he was relieved he laid down on the wet marshy ground along the bank of Bayou's. Across the water on the opposite bank lay the enemy's picket. He was certain the disease was contracted there, and subsequently on the exposure on General Banks expedition up the Red River. In 1865 it was in his right hip and knee and he was subject to attacks of increased severity, disabling him from doing manual labor. In 1867 he went north to Mazomanie, where he still suffered from rheumatism. When he left the service, he lived in New Orleans, Louisiana; Mazomanie and Seneca, Wisconsin. In 1882 he raised poultry, but was unable to feed them. The disease affected him most in the winter season and he felt excruciating pain, most severe when he was not able to purchase suitable under clothing. In 1882 he was living at the Soldiers Home in Milwaukee, age 63, height 5'9", weight 150 pounds, light complexion. [115]

Ben Parkin

---

[113] Wisconsin Adjutant General, Regimental Descriptive Rolls 1861-1865, 11rd Infantry, Company A. (FHL #1311670)

[114] National Archives, Washington D.C., Pension File: Benjamin Parkin, Company A, 11th Wisconsin Infantry, invalid pension on 5 May 1882, application #448435, certificate #338854, filed in Wisconsin.

Porter, John F. Private - Company E, 23rd Wisconsin
He enlisted as a private in Company E, 23rd Regiment, 4 January 1864 at Mazomanie by W. Brink for three years. He mustered in 9 January 1864 at Madison, age 25, gray eyes, dark hair, light complexion, 5'8", a farmer from Mazomanie, Dane, Wisconsin. The enemy captured him at Sabine Cross Roads and was a prisoner at Tyler, Texas. He died 12 September 1864 from chronic diarrhea at Camp Tyler, Texas and buried Alexandria, Louisiana, section 18, grave 58.[116]

Porter, David Dixon   Rear Admiral
He was born in 1813 and began his naval career sailing with his father in the West Indies. He was a commissioned midshipman, first in the Mexican navy, joining the United States Navy in 1829. During the Mexican War he served in the Gulf, the South Atlantic, and the Mediterranean. Porter gave distinguished service in the Civil War, first at Vicksburg, and later with the North Atlantic squadron. In 1866 they promoted him vice admiral and given superintendency of the Naval Academy. Grant appointed him a special advisor to the Navy Department, where Porter made many administrative reforms. He succeeded Farragut as admiral in 1870, serving on the board of Inspection until his death in 1891. The papers of David Porter and David Dixon Porter, American naval officers are at the William Clements Library at the University of Michigan. The collection contains approximately 250 items relating to David Porter, 1805-1840; most of them deal with his War of 1812 service and his West Indian duty, but some are on the Mexican navy and his diplomatic career. One hundred and twenty-five items are concerning the career of David D. Porter. Two autobiographical manuscripts, 'My Career in the Navy Department' and portions of a journal describing his Civil War experiences, are included, as well as a number of literary manuscripts, fragments of novels, essays, speeches, and biographical notes.[117]

---

[115] Wisconsin Adjutant General, Regimental Descriptive Rolls 1861-1865, 23rd Infantry, Company E. (FHL #1311689)

[116] William L. Clements Library, The University of Michigan, David and David D. Porter Papers, *Papers, 1805-1908, 4 lin. feet.*

David D. Porter

Quigley, George W. Private - Company E, 23rd Wisconsin
He was born 3 April 1840 in Lockport, New York, the son of Vantile Quigley & Kathern Stucker of New York. He came to Oregon, Wisconsin in 1861. On 14 August 1862 at Oregon, James M. Bull enlisted him for three years as a private, in Company E, 23rd Wisconsin. He mustered in 30 August 1862 at Madison. He was single, 22 years, his home was Oregon, Dane County, Wisconsin and he mustered out with company, 4 July 1865 at Mobile, Alabama.

He married Lavina Brader on 9 January 1866 in Elgon, Wisconsin. He went to Iowa in October 1869, and settled on a farm in Kendrick Township. He moved to Scranton in November 1890. He applied for an invalid pension on 25 March 1880. In 1902 he was receiving a pension of $6.00 per month, due to lumbago, piles, rheumatism. He was then 62 years of age; height 5'7 ½," weight 170 pounds, dark complexion, brown eyes, black hair and his occupation was attending horses. His back was injured in the Spring of 1864 at Sabine Cross Roads, Louisiana and he was three-quarters disabled for earning his subsistence by manual labor. The injury was due to being trod on by horses and he could not farm or do other heavy work. In 1885 Frank B Webb's affidavit states that on or about 8 April 1864 at Sabine Cross Roads in Louisiana, George *was hurt and seriously injured by being run over, trampled upon and hurt by a body of Rebel mounted infantry while on a retreat on the Bank's Expedition from up the Red River, the union forces there being whipped and retreating in disorder. The claimant was then and there placed upon a horse and helped to camp where he was treated by an assistant surgeon, Dr. Wood.* In an affidavit by Daniel J. Jenks, in 1885, he stated that George worked for him driving a team and that it was nearly all the work he was able to do. He also stated that he would not pay him half price unless he worked with a team. He earns what he lives on by teaming and the help of a son, 18 years old. *He can not alone earn his living and is a worthy man and should have a pension.*

He had the following children: Eva, born 9 August 1866; William O. born 9 August 1868, died 21 December 1908; John V., born 5 March 1873, died 1956; Peter/Betsy(?), born 19 November 1874; George E., born 2 November 1876, died 1950; Edney, born 16 March 1888. George Quigley, of Company E, was living in Scranton City, Iowa in 1889 and he attended both reunions of the 23rd Wisconsin, the first at Madison 15-16 September 1886 and the second at Milwaukee, 28

August 1889. He lived in Scranton and vicinity for 45 years, settling there shortly after they established the Northwestern railroad. Mr. Quigley maintained a reputation second to none for business integrity, and they remembered him as his word was good. He was a good neighbor, a true friend, and a kind and considerate husband and father. He did not belong to a church. They christened him in infancy in the Episcopal church, but he believed in the doctrine of the Universalist church. He was a retired farmer, who died in Scranton, Greene County, Iowa of uremic poison on 24 February 1914. The contributory cause was Bright's disease. He was ill only ten days and the news of his death came as a severe shock to his friends. They conducted funeral services from the Christian church, where friends and relatives filled every seat in the church. The Grand Army flag was at half mast during the day and his comrades were in charge of his funeral. He was buried in the Scranton Township Cemetery along with his wife and children. His widow, Lavina Quigley (1840-1919), filed for her widow pension on 4 March 1914. [118]

George Quigley

---

[117] Wisconsin Adjutant General, Regimental Descriptive Rolls 1861-1865, 23rd Infantry, Company E. (FHL #1311689); National Archives, Washington D.C., Pension File: George W. Quigley, Company E, 23rd Wisconsin Infantry, invalid pension filed: 25 Mar 1880, application #353707, certificate #324198. Lavina Quigley widow pension filed: 4 Mar 1914, application #1023283, certificate #774647, filed in Iowa; *Scranton Township Cemetery, Greene County, Iowa*, compiled by Greene County Genealogical Society, 1895) p.20, 81; Civil War Unit Histories, Part 4, The Union-Midwest and West: Regimental Histories and Personal Narratives. *The Survivors of the Twenty-third Regiment Wisconsin Volunteer Infantry*, 1889; Obituary *Scranton Journal*, 26 Feb 1914.

Ransom, Thomas Edward Greenfield   Brigadier-General
He was born 29 November 1834 in Norwich, Vermont, the son of Truman Bishop Ransom and Margaret. They educated him at Newbury seminary and Norwich University. Early in 1861 he recruited a company for the 11th Illinois regiment and he was commissioned captain on April 24. He became Major of the regiment in June and Lieutenant-Colonel on July 30. He became colonel of his regiment on 15 February 1862. He became chief of staff to General McClernand and inspector-general of the Army of the Tennessee in June. They promoted him brigadier-general of the volunteers in January 1863. In the Red River campaign he commanded a division and received a wound in the knee at Sabine Cross Roads, from which he never recovered. Both Grant and Sherman pronounced General Ransom to be among the ablest generals on their commands. He died on 29 October in Rome, Georgia, from illness brought on by over work and exposure. [119]

Thomas Edward Greenfield Ransom

---

[118] *The Union Army* (Broadfoot Publishing Company; Wilmington, NC, 1998) vol. 8:42; International Genealogical Index version 4.01.

Reynolds, Joseph Jones Major-General
He was born 4 January 1822 in Flemingsburg, Kentucky, the son of Edward Reynolds and Sarah Ann Longley. When he was 15, his family moved across the Ohio River to Lafayette, Indiana. At 16, he entered Wabash College at Crawfordsville, and, a year later they appointed him to West Point. He graduated from the military academy in 1843, tenth in a class of 39. The class of 1843, also included General Grant. He was an assistant professor at the academy from 1846 until 1849, then a principal assistant professor of natural and experimental philosophy until 1855. After garrison duty and serving in the military occupation of Texas just before the war with Mexico, they assigned him as instructor at West Point, where he taught for eight years. He then did frontier duty in the Indian Territory until he resigned as First Lieutenant, 3rd U.S. Artillery, in 1857. He taught engineering at St. Louis University before returning to Lafayette to operate a grocery business with his brother. With the outbreak of the Civil War in April 1861, he was commissioned colonel of the three-month 10th Indiana Volunteer Infantry Regiment. Less than two months later, they promoted him to brigadier general of volunteers and assigned to a department command in (West) Virginia. The following December his brother died, and he resigned his commission and returned to Lafayette to supervise the family business. He was re-commissioned in September 1862 and in November was promoted to major general of volunteers. In 1863 he commanded several divisions. In November, he was made George Thomas's chief of staff, when they ordered him back to line duty in January 1864. From late 1864 until early 1866 he commanded the Department of Arkansas and he received two brevet commissions for gallant and meritorious service in the Civil War. Named to the regular army rank of colonel in 1866, he served in the infantry until 1870 when he transferred to the command of cavalry troops. In 1871 he was elected to the U.S. Senate by the carpetbag legislature in Texas, but the brother of General A. J. Hamilton successfully contested the seat. He next commanded at various points in Nebraska and Wyoming. He was commanding the advance of George Crook's expedition when it attacked and captured the Sioux village on the Powder River, 17 March 1876. He prematurely ordered a retreat, leaving his dead and a wounded Private in the hands of Indians who "promptly cut the Private limb from limb." His career was ruined and he resigned the next year and moved to Washington, D.C., where he died on 25 February 1899. He was buried in Section 1, Grave 82-C, Arlington National Cemetery. His wife, Mary E. Bainbridge Reynolds (1827-1913) is buried with

him. [120]

Joseph Jones Reynolds

<u>Rice, Samuel G.</u>   Private - Company E, 23rd Wisconsin
He was born at Ashtabula County, Ohio, the son of Gardiner and Fanny Rice. In 1848 his parents went to Oregon, Wisconsin, from Ohio. He enlisted in Company E, 23rd Wisconsin Infantry on 5 July 1862 at Madison, Wisconsin and was discharged 17 May 1865. At the time of enlistment he was 22, single. He applied for an invalid pension on 7 June 1880. Before his enlistment he was a farmer. Samuel's first wife died in Oregon, Wisconsin on 17 May 1869. Samuel G. Rice married second, Hannah West at Oregon, Dane County, Wisconsin on 11 September 1873. Hannah West was born 11 Jan 1841 at West Haddon, England, the daughter of John and Mary Anne West. They had one son less than 16 years of age when Samuel died, John S. Rice was born 18 May 1879. After the war Samuel was treated for heart disease caused from the forced March and heavy cartridges on his belt. He worked for his father, then after December 1865 he worked in

---

[119] *The Union Army* (Broadfoot Publishing Company; Wilmington, NC, 1998) vol. 8; International Genealogical Index, version 4.01; Indiana in the Civil War; Arlington National Cemetery Website: http://www.arlingtoncemetery.com/jjreynold.htm.

Oregon village with the intent of learning the tin trade from Mr. Cowler, until November 1867. After that for J. B. Gardner, in Oregon, for $4 dollars a week for forty weeks, when other able men got $16 per week. He then started a tin shop in the same place and did the light work and hired the heavy work. His health then failed in 1868, which was written in his diary. His diary was destroyed in May 1875 when a cyclone blew his house down and he lost most his household goods. His father had given him a 13-acre plot on one end of his farm. The county gave him money to build again and he was making a garden when my cow got out of the pasture in the garden. When he was driving the cow back, he was bare footed, he stepped on a crab apple brush and got a thorn in the bottom of his foot that he never got out. It worked up through the top of his foot so that he could not do all of his garden work. His neighbor finished the garden and Dr. George Fox cut open his foot stating that it was a group of ulcers. He was laid up for five weeks when his wife rubbed some of Kelloggs King of Pain for "nervous head ache" and chills and it healed his foot. He left Oregon because he father died and he missed his parent's help, as his wife got sick and she could not do her needlework as she was accustomed to doing to earn a living. He sold out and started a tin shop but he could not work more than half the time.

He was living in Verona, Wisconsin in 1899. He attended both reunions of the 23rd Wisconsin, the first at Madison 15-16 September 1886 and the second at Milwaukee, 28 August 1889. Samuel died 18 January 1896 and his widow, Hannah R. Rice, filed for her widow pension on 18 February 1898. Hannah married second Levi H. Mahama on 6 October 1902 at Washington, D.C. and obtained judgment of divorce from him on 21 March 1904. Then she did not have any kind of property nor income. She was admitted to membership of the Wisconsin Veterans Home on 19 March 1902 from the City of Oshkosh, Wisconsin. She was without any means of support other than provided by the State of Wisconsin. Hannah married third on 14 November 1905 to Joseph Watson at Waupaca, Wisconsin. Joseph Watson died 4 August 1913 at Oregon, Wisconsin. Joseph Watson served in the U.S. Navy. [121]

---

[120] National Archives, Washington D.C., Pension File: Samuel G. Rice, Company E, 23rd Wisconsin Infantry, invalid pension filed: 7 Jun 1880, application #372062, certificate #383007. Hannah R. Rice widow pension filed: 18 Feb 1898, application #570813, certificate #407743, filed in Wisconsin; Civil War Unit Histories,

Samuel G. Rice [signature]

Roberts, Hugh Private - Company E, 23rd Wisconsin
On 15 August 1862 at Madison, James M. Bull enlisted him for three years, in Company E, 23rd Regiment. He mustered in 30 August 1862 at Madison, single, 22 years old, home: Berry, Dane County. They appointed him Corporal 1 April 1863, Sergeant 12 February 1864, reduced to ranks 21 April 1865. They discharged him 24 May 1865. [122]

Roche, Leon J. Corporal - Company E, 23rd Wisconsin
He was born 28 October 1839, and a native of Local, Switzerland who came to America at the age of nine. On 14 April 1862 at Mazomanie, James M. Bull enlisted him for three years, in Company E, 23rd Wisconsin Infantry. He mustered as corporal in Company E, 23rd Wisconsin on 30 August 1862 at Madison, single, age 23. They appointed him Sergeant on 1 April 1863, reduced to ranks 21 March 1865. He was wounded on 11 January 1863 at Arkansas Post, Arkansas and on 8 April 1864 at Sabine Cross Roads, Louisiana.

He applied for an invalid pension on 24 Jan 1872 when he was 33 years old, 5'9", weight 150 pounds. He had a rupture on his left side, which he wore a truss. James M. Bull, former Captain of Company E, 23rd Wisconsin stated that Leon's rupture happened on a night march made up a high and very steep hill near Newport, Kentucky sometime among the first and middle of September 1862.

Leon married Anna Wisch on 24 September 1868 at Alexandria, Clark county, Missouri. When he was 51 years old he was 5' 8 ½," weight 136. He had a wound to the right hand, a ball passed through middle of his ring finger, fracturing the bone. The ball passed over the last joint

---

Part 4, The Union- Midwest and West: Regimental Histories and Personal Narratives.
The Survivors of the Twenty-third Regiment Wisconsin Volunteer Infantry, 1889.
[121] Wisconsin Adjutant General, Regimental Descriptive Rolls 1861-1865, 23rd Infantry, Company E. (FHL #1311689)

of the little finger resulting in the finger sticking straight out and his ring finger is permanently flexed at second joint. He was living in Warsaw, Illinois in 1889, but he did not attend the reunions of the 23rd Wisconsin Regiment in 1886 or 1889. He died at Keokuk, Iowa 30 June 1898. *He died at 2:30 o'clock at his home, 221 North Tenth street, was a profound shock to the people of this community where he was well known. His illness was very brief and many of his friends knew nothing of it until the tidings of his death came. The cause of death was strangulation of the bowels. He was down town as late as Tuesday, and while complaining somewhat, gave no evidence of serious illness. He was survived by his wife and four children: Louis J. Roche, Mrs. Geo. S. Tucker, Clara J. Roche and Robert G. Roche. Three sisters also mourn his loss, Mrs. Henry Loche of Burlingotn, Mrs. Adele Ketterer of Omaha, and Miss Martha Roach of Omaha. He was affiliated with the lodge of Odd Fellows at Warsaw and was an exemplary citizen, a brave soldier, the head of a happy home, and a man whose good qualities survive to make him many friends. Following the example of his father, his son, Robert G. Roche, enlisted for the present war and is a member of Company A, Fiftieth Iowa volunteers, in Camp Cuba Libre at Jacksonville. Word was sent to him and if a furlough can be secured he will return for the funeral.* He was a member of the G. A. R. and I. O. O. F. His widow, Anna Roche, filed for her widow pension on 9 July 1898. Anna Roche died 6 August 1927. [123]

---

[122] Wisconsin Adjutant General, Regimental Descriptive Rolls 1861-1865, 23rd Infantry, Company E. (FHL #1311689); National Archives, Washington D.C., Pension File: Leon J. Roche, Company E, 23 Wisconsin Infantry, invalid pension, certificate #123686; Anna Roche widow pension; Civil War Unit Histories, Part 4, The Union- Midwest and West: Regimental Histories and Personal Narratives. *The Survivors of the Twenty-third Regiment Wisconsin Volunteer Infantry*, 1889; Obituary: Gate City, 6 July 1898.

Schlick, Jacob A. Captain - Company F, 23rd Wisconsin
He was born 1 April 1839 in Danville, Livingston County, New York, the son of Nicholas Schlick. When he was eighteen years old, he served a three year apprenticeship to a blacksmith. He thought a change of climate would *prove beneficial to his health* and he moved to Wisconsin. He was a Captain, commissioned 30 August 1862 by the Governor of Wisconsin, age 23. Mustered in as 2nd Lieutenant 15 August 1862 at Madison, served in Company A, 6th & Company F, 23 Wisconsin Infantry, his home was Baraboo, Sauk County. At the time of enlistment he was 22 years old, 5'7 ½," light complexion, hazel eyes, auburn hair, he was a miller. He mustered out on 4 July 1865. Action: Chickasaw Bayou; Arkansas Post, Champion Hills, Black River Bridge; Siege of Vicksburg; Carrion Crow Bayou; Sabine Cross Roads. He filed for an invalid pension on 15 November 1879. After leaving the service he lived near Baraboo, Wisconsin until November 1868; Decatur, Michigan until November 1872 and Bennington, New York. On 6 July 1865, he was officer of the day and while in the line of duty at New Orleans, while they were taking coal on board the steamboat on which the regiment was embarked, an intoxicated soldier on the gang plank threw or pushed him of the steamer, striking the small of his back on the edge of the plank, nearly producing a fracture of the spine and causing internal injuries. The incident was so serious that the colonel of the 23rd regiment (Colonel Guppy) noted it in his memorandum book.

He was a well-known resident of Bennington, where he owed a farm of one hundred and sixty-two acres. After Jacob's death, his eldest son, Frank A. Schlick carried on general farming and dairying. Florence E. Day was born 17 October 1847 at Bennington, New York and married Jacob A. Schlick on 23 October 1866 at Attica, Wyoming, New York. They had three children; Frank, Volney and Agnes. In politics he was a straight Republican and he was reared to the Catholic faith, but *he did not adher to the doctrines of that church.* He was living in Bennington, New York in 1889 and he attended the second reunion for the 23rd Wisconsin at Milwaukee, 28 August 1889. He was a member of the Rowley P. Taylor Post, G.A.R. Jacob died 7 March 1920 at Attica, New York and is buried at Bennington Center. His widow, Florence E Schlick, filed for her widow pension on 17 March 1920. [124]

---

[123] National Archives, Washington D.C., Pension File: Jacob A. Schlick, Company A, 6th & Company F, 23 Wisconsin Infantry, invalid pension filed: 15 Nov 1879, application #323188, certificate #205559. Florence E Schlick widow pension

Jacob H. Schick
(Claimant's signature in full.)

Sickles, Daniel Edgar   Major General

He was born on October 20, 1819 in New York City, the son of a well-to-do patent lawyer. He repeatedly ran away from home. They sent him to a boarding school at the age of fifteen failed when he fought with a teacher. After a year long stint as a printer's helper, he returned to New York City and began developing his lifestyle, hanging out with prostitutes and other unsavory characters. His parents sent him to live with a mentor, Lorenzo Da Pont, who prepared him for college. After a year with Da Pont, Sickles entered New York University, but when Da Pont died suddenly, Sickles left college to study law. At the same time he began his long association with Tammany Hall politics in New York City. In 1843, at the age of twenty-four, he was admitted to the bar, and soon made himself notorious in Tammany politics while developing a reputation as a high liver. He was elected to the New York State Assembly in 1847, advancing his political career despite such high-profile escapades as escorting prostitutes into the legislative chambers. In 1852 he married, against the will of both families, she was sixteen and he was twice her age.

He spent a year abroad as secretary to the minister to Great Britain. He scandalized the host country by refusing to toast to the health of Queen Victoria at an Independence Day banquet. Returning to America, Sickles was elected state senator in 1855, then a member of Congress in 1856. At that point, Sickles, a militia officer and student of military affairs, clearly had his sights set on nothing less than the Presidency. He lived far beyond his means, continued his lecherous indiscretions, and made himself a notorious figure in Washington society. Then in 1859 came the Philip Barton Key incident. Key was the son of the

---

filed: 17 Mar 1920, application #1154488, certificate #888429, filed in New York; *Livingston and Wyoming County Biographical Review of Leading Citizens* (Boston Biographical Review Publishing Company, 1895), p. 104-105; Civil War Unit Histories, Part 4, The Union- Midwest and West: Regimental Histories and Personal Narratives. *The Survivors of the Twenty-third Regiment Wisconsin Volunteer Infantry*, 1889; Wisconsin Adjutant General, Regimental Descriptive Rolls 1861-1865, 23rd Infantry, Company F.   (FHL #1311689).

author of "The Star-Spangled Banner," a militia captain, political dabbler, and man-about-town in the capital, where they knew him as *the handsomest man in all Washington society*. Key had legal business with Sickles, and after a while began seeing Sickles's wife in a shabby apartment. Sickles found out and shot him dead, in Lafayette Park, across the street from the White House. After shooting Key, Sickles walked down the street and surrendered himself to the Attorney General of the United States. At his murder trial, a phalanx of lawyers defended Sickles. They entered, for the first time in history, the plea of "temporary insanity." Washington was essentially a Southern town, a place where they might take a man seriously if he claimed to be driven mad by the shock of his wife betraying him with his friend. After a circus trial, they acquitted Sickles. He returned to New York and had just resumed practicing law when the war broke out in April 1861. He decided to raise a regiment, as men who mustered in the most men stood the best chance of getting a brigadier general's star from Congress. Sickles soon had raised an entire brigade, dubbing it the "Excelsior Brigade." Sickles considered it his brigade, independent of New York state authority. As an independent military organization, it was supposed to pay its own way, and debts began piling up immediately. Sickles got permission to move part of the brigade to Staten Island, and managed to get a loan of a circus tent from P.T. Barnum to provide shelter. Another fourteen hundred men were quartered in a bare hall on lower Broadway. Sickles contracted with a bathhouse to give them all a shower and shave at ten cents each. Sickles pestered Lincoln and everyone he knew in Washington to swear his troop in as United States volunteers. The governor of New York was outraged and tried to disband the brigade. It required a general order from the Secretary of War to place the Excelsior Brigade under the governor's control. The regiments became the 70th, 71st, 72nd, 73rd, and 74th New York Volunteers. After 1st Bull Run, with Washington embattled and crying out for more troops, they put Sickles's brigade on a train for the capital, and soon became part of the then-forming Army of the Potomac. Sickles boarded the train and left behind somewhere between $250,000 and $400,000 in debts owed by the brigade. Meanwhile, Sickles himself was sworn into the army at the beginning rank of brigadier general. At the end of his life, he became separated not only from family but from reality and died on 3 May 1914 at his home in New York City. He is buried in Section 2 of

Arlington National Cemetery.

Daniel Edgar Sic kles

Smith, Andrew Jackson   Major General
He was born 28 April 1815 in Bucks County, Pennsylvania. He was a Major-General, cadet at the U.S. Military academy from 1834-1838, when he graduated and was promoted in the army to second lieutenant in the 1st dragoons. He served on the frontier and served in the Civil war, first as colonel of the 2nd California Calvary, then chief of the calvary. He was commissioned brigadier-general of volunteers in March 1862 and he was in the expedition to Arkansas Post in January 1863. He was in the Vicksburg campaign from January to July, commanding a division in the 13th army corps. He was engaged in the advance to Grand Gulf, the battles of Port Gibson, Champion's Hill, Big Black river, assaults on Vicksburg and the seize. He was in command of the 6th division, 16th army Corps from August 1863 until January 1864. He was in the Red River Campaign, commanding detachments of the 16th and 17th army corps March 6 to May 22. He was engaged in the assault and capture of Fort De Russy and the battle of Pleasant Hill. He died 30 January 1897 in St. Louis, Missouri.

---

[124] Arlington National Cemetery Website: http://www.arlingtoncemetery.com/dsickles.htm; http://www.civilwarhome.com/sicklesbio.htm

[125] The Union Army (Broadfoot Publishing Company: Wilmington, NC, 1998) v. 8:42

Andrew Jackson Smith

Sumner, John Milton
He was born 26 June 1838 in Tifflin, Ohio. His parents, James and Jane Sumner went to Madison in 1856 and John followed them the next year. Wayne Ramsay employed him, then in the hardware business. He enlisted as a private, then at the end of his enlistment, he reenlisted in Company I of the 23rd Wisconsin Regiment. He was second lieutenant of the company, then was promoted to first lieutenant of Company B, and later became captain. They commissioned him 21 August 1862, to second lieutenant, by Governor of Wisconsin for three years, 24, single. He mustered in on 30 August 1862 at Madison. He was commissioned Captain of Company D, 23rd Regiment, 31 October 1863 at Ibina, Louisiana, age 25, home Madison. He mustered out on 4 July 1865. Engagements: Port Gibson; Champion Hills; Black River Bridge; Siege of Vicksburg; Jackson, Miss; Carrion Crow Bayou; Sabine Cross Roads.

He returned to the hardware business after the civil war and was the senior partner of Sumner & Morris. He served in B, D & I, 23 and K 1 Wisconsin infantry and filed for an invalid pension on 18 May 1904. He was living in Madison, Wisconsin in 1889. He attended both reunions of the 23rd Wisconsin, the first at Madison 15-16 September 1886 and the second at Milwaukee, 28 August 1889. He retired from business in 1918. He was one of the three oldest members of the Madison Masonic Lodge and was a member of the G. A. R. He died 30

March 1922 at his home in Madison, 13 North Hancock street. He had been a resident since 1857 and had engaged in the hardware business for more than fifty years. He was one of Madison's old settlers, dying of old age. He left one son, John Douglas Sumner of Madison; and three daughters, Mrs. H. L. Mosley, Madison; Mrs. Thomas A. Sanderson, Sturgeon Bay, Wisconsin; Mrs. Damon A. Brown, Peoria, Illinois. Funeral services were conducted at his home by George E. Hunt, pastor of Christ Presbyterian Church. The G.A. R. conducted the services at the grave in Forest Hill. His widow, Mary Woodward Sumner, filed her widow pension on 7 April 1922.[127]

Tolford, Joshua Woodbury Captain - Company G, 23rd Wisconsin
He was born 1 October 1831 in Woodstock, New Jersey. When he was seventeen, he went to Portland, Maine where he learned the trade of carriage painter. In 1852 he went to Madison where he worked at his trade. He enlisted on 21 August 1862 as First Lieutenant and mustered in 30 August 1862. He was married, age 31, and his residence was Madison. They promoted him Captain of Company G, 23rd Wisconsin infantry. He saw the following action: Chickasaw Bayou; Arkansas Port; Port Gibson; Champion Hills; Black River Bridge; Siege of Vicksburg; Carrion Crow Bayou; Sabine Cross Roads. He mustered out 4 July 1865. He filed for an invalid pension on 15 December 1892. After his discharge he lived at Madison until July 1872 where he engaged in business and was Chief of Police. He then moved to Nellsville, Wisconsin where he went into a livery and stage business. The firm operated a four-horse coach between Neillsville and Humbird. In 1903, he was 5'9", weight 157 pounds, grey eyes, grey hair, dark complexion. His disability was caused near Vicksburg, Mississippi on or about 1 January 1863 when he was disabled by chronic diarrhea followed by piles and rheumatism and disease of the feet and varicose

---

[126] Wisconsin Adjutant General, Regimental Descriptive Rolls, 1861-1865, 23rd Infantry, Company D and Company E;
Organization index to pension files of veterans, Company K, 1st WI, B & I, 23rd WI; National Archives, Washington D.C., Pension File: John M. Sumner, Company K, 1st WI, B & I, , 23rd Wisconsin Infantry, invalid pension filed: application #1316440, certificate #10942723, filed in Wisconsin, Mary Woodward Sumner, widow pension, application #1187871, certificate #916928, XC 2706478, filed in Wisconsin; Civil War Unit Histories, Part 4, The Union- Midwest and West: Regimental Histories and Personal Narratives. *The Survivors of the Twenty-third Regiment Wisconsin Volunteer Infantry*, 1889; Obituary, *Wisconsin State Journal*, 30 March 1922.

veins on the march from Jackson, Mississippi to Vicksburg.

He married Julia E. Jewett on 29 September 1859 in Madison. They had six children; Arthur died in 1864, Frank in 1866, Minnie in 1908 and a baby in 1874. Two sons survived him, Ralph of Thorp and Joshua W. Jr. of Jerome, Arizona. Joshua was living in Neillsville, Wisconsin in 1889 and he attended the 23rd Wisconsin's reunion in Madison 15-16 September 1886. He took a leading part in building a telegraph line from Neillsville to Hatfield. He served as Sheriff and later was assistant Clerk of the Circuit Court. He was one of the oldest Freemasons in Wisconsin, joining the order in 1853. For many years he remained a member of the Madison lodge, but attended and worked with the Neillsville lodge. He was the first commander of the Lucius Fairchild Post of the Grand Army of the Republic (the first G. A. R. Post organized) and took an active part in that organization. He also organized the Sherman Guards, the first militia company in Neillsville and was their first captain. Joshua died 20 December 1913 in Neillsville, Clark County, Wisconsin and he was buried December 23rd in Madison. He died of sclerosis of coronary arteries of the heart and his widow, Julia E. Tolford filed for her pension on 12 January 1914. [128]

---

[127] National Archives, Washington D.C., Pension File: Joshua Tolford, Company G, 23rd Wisconsin Infantry, invalid pension files: 15 Dec 1892, application $1141479, certificate #1076033, filed in Wisconsin, Julia E. Tolford widow pension filed: 12 Jan 1914, application $1020372, certificate #771250, filed in Wisconsin; Obituary [newspaper name & date not noted]; Civil War Unit Histories, Part 4, The Union- Midwest and West: Regimental Histories and Personal Narratives. *The Survivors of the Twenty-third Regiment Wisconsin Volunteer Infantry*, 1889.

Tyker, John G.   Sergeant - Company E, 23rd Wisconsin
He was born in Schoharie County, New York in 1832. In 1835 he moved to Ohio with his parents and to Illinois in 1837. His father drowned in the Pecatonica River and he went to Iowa County, Wisconsin in 1845. On 14 August 1862 at Rutland, Joseph Dejean enlisted him for three years, as a sergeant of Company E, 23rd Wisconsin. He mustered in 30 August 1862 in Madison, single, 30 years old, his home was Mazomanie, Dane County. He was appointed corporal on 1 April 1863, promoted sergeant on 9 August 1863, reduced to ranks from sergeant on 21 March 1865. He mustered out with the company 4 July 1865 at Mobile, Alabama.

He filed for an invalid pension on 11 November 1890. John F. Calkins, of the 23rd regiment, stated in an affidavit that he was well acquainted with John G. Tyler. He knew that in the spring of 1864, John Tyler had been to the State of Wisconsin as a recruiter. When he returned to the regiment he had the chronic diarrhea and in the fall of the same year he became sick with the jaundice. He did not do duty for four or five weeks. The Regimental surgeon treated him, but he was never quite well. In the winter of 1864 and spring of 1865 while they were in Helena, Arkansas he had malarial fever and was unable to do duty. He was overcome by malaria and jaundice due to the companies last march, April 1865, through the swamps of southern Alabama, on the Mobile Campaign and the capture of Spanish Fort and Fort Blalcaly. *The march was severe in the extreme owing to the disadvantages with which we had to contend. No shelter, poor water and had to carry shovels, axes and spades to build roads in __ our progress. Sickness and disease overcame many soldiers, including John G. Tyler,* as stated by the musician of Company E, 23rd Wisconsin, Porter Learurel. His farm in Mazomanie was about 200 acres. He married Amelia Watson, the daughter of William A. and Martha Watson, on 11 January 1866 at Arena, Wisconsin. He died 9 July 1892, at the village of Dover, Wisconsin, of malarial fever aggravated and caused by chronic diarrhea and jaundice. He also suffered from piles and lumbago. They had one child, Reginald Tyler, born 7 October 1881. He was living in Mazomanie in 1889. He attended both reunions of the 23rd Wisconsin, the first at Madison 15-16 September 1886 and the second at

Milwaukee, 28 August 1889. [129]

Webb, Franklin   Corporal - Company E, 23rd Wisconsin
He was born 3 March 1843, at Lima, Rock County, Wisconsin, the son of Clark Webb and Alvira Coats of New York State. On 11 August 1862 at Montrose, James M. Bull enlisted him for three years, as a corporal in Company E, 23rd Wisconsin. He mustered in 30 August 1862 at Madison. He was single, 19 years old, 5'9", light complexion, blue eyes, brown hair and was a farmer in Montrose. He mustered out with the company, 4 July 1865 at Mobile, Alabama. He was appointed corporal 12 February 1864, reduced to ranks 21 March 1865. Franklin Webb was absent, due to dysentery, in General Hospital, New Orleans, Louisiana from August 1864 until September. He filed for an invalid pension on 16 November 1881. He was living in Kendall, Wisconsin in 1889 and he attended the 23rd Wisconsin's reunion in Madison 15-16 September 1886.

He married Hannah H. Chatterton, on 1 March 1870 at Oregon, Dane County, Wisconsin. He filed for an invalid pension on 16 November 1881. Hannah, in 1922 was a resident of Elroy, where she attended to her husband, due to his partial blindness, deafness and feebleness caused by old age. She helped him to his feet when he fell, helped dress him and waited on him generally. She died 3 August 1927 and he married Hattie R., born 19 July 1863, the widow of James Webb, who died at Belleville, Wisconsin about 3 February 1924. She married Franklin Webb on 19 May 1928 at Rockford, Illinois. She had one family member who served in the Army between 1917 and 1921, Ira L. Webb. He was a private, enlisting 29 August 1918 at Carrington, North Dakota and was discharged 19 July 1919. He was living in St. Paul, Minnesota in 1937. Franklin Webb was in the National Home, Wisconsin for about two and one-half months. He filed his declaration for pension citing that he was unable to perform manual labor by

---

[128] Wisconsin Adjutant General, Regimental Descriptive Rolls 1861-1865, 23rd Wisconsin, Company E; National Archives, Washington D.C., Pension File: John G. Tyler, Company E, 23rd Wisconsin Infantry, invalid pension filed: 11 Nov 1890, application #974169, certificate #896674, filed in Wisconsin; *History of Iowa County, Wisconsin: containing an account f its settlement, growth, development and resources, biographical sketches* (Chicago: Western Historical Co., 1881.); Civil War Unit Histories, Part 4, The Union- Midwest and West: Regimental Histories and Personal Narratives. *The Survivors of the Twenty-third Regiment Wisconsin Volunteer Infantry*, 1889.

reason of injury and diseases incurred in the line of duty, rupture, diarrhea, eyes and lungs. In 1922 it was reported that he had total loss of sight in his left eye. His right eye *nearly so, both due to cataract. An operation was performed on his left eye, but he was expected to have total blindness shortly. His hearing was very defective. It was necessary to be helped about much of the time.* When he left the service, he lived in Dane County, Wisconsin from 1865 to 1883; Monroe County, Wisconsin from 1883 to 1904; Elroy, Wisconsin 1904 to 1907; Dunn County North Dakota 1907 to 1909, and Elroy, Wisconsin. In 1915 he listed the following children: Amy Webb, born 11 March 1873, died 8 January 1879; Fannie Eugine Champlain born 18 March 1875; Ruth Smith born 10 May 1877, died 20 January 1910; Clark Webb born 16 December 1880; Clarence C. Webb born 30 July 1885; Claude W. Webb born 24 June 1890. Franklin Webb died 5 January 1937 at Elroy, Juneau, Wisconsin. They held funeral services at the Elroy Methodist Church. He was a farmer, survived by his wife, Hattie R. Webb, buried in Mt. Tabor Cemetery. They listed the cause of death as senility, due to cardiac failure. [130]

---

[129] Wisconsin Adjutant General, Regimental Descriptive Rolls 1861-1865, 23rd Wisconsin, Company E; National Archives, Washington D.C., Pension File: Franklin Webb, Company E, 23rd Wisconsin Infantry, invalid pension filed 16 Nov 1881, application #433516, certificatre #279990, filed in Wisconsin. CZ575074; Civil War Unit Histories, Part 4, The Union- Midwest and West: Regimental Histories and Personal Narratives. *The Survivors of the Twenty-third Regiment Wisconsin Volunteer Infantry*, 1889; Obituary *Elroy Leader-Tribune* 14 January 1937.

Wheeler, Ira H.   Private - Company E, 23rd Wisconsin
On 14 January 1864 at Mazomanie, J. G. Tyler enlisted him for three years, as a private in Company E, 23rd Wisconsin. He mustered in 19 January 1864 at Madison. He was 32 years old, blue eyes, light hair, light complexion, 5'10", farmer. He transferred to Company I, 35th Wisconsin on 4 July 1865 at Mobile, Alabama. Battles: Siege of Spanish Fort and Blakely, Alabama.

He married Nancy M. Soles on 7 September 1850 at Albian, New York. He died on 17 July 1868 at Druan, Illinois. His widow, Nancy M. Wheeler, applied for her widow pension on 4 August 1890 when she was living at North 1935 St., Gerome Park, Denver, Colorado. In 1891 E. L. and Rosa Jones stated that Nancy had not remarried since the death of her late husband. She had no means of support only her own daily labor and that she had no real or personal estate. She had lived with them since 1883.[131]

---

[130] Wisconsin Adjutant General, Regimental Descriptive Rolls 1861-1865, 23rd Wisconsin, Company E; National Archives, Washington D.C., Pension File: Ira H. Wheeler, Company E, 23rd Wisconsin Infantry and Company I, 35th Wisconsin, Nancy M. Wheeler widow pension filed: 4 Aug 1890, application #474471, certificate #377924, filed in Colorado.

Wikoff, Jacob C.   Private - Company E, 23rd Wisconsin

He was born in Philadelphia about 1835. On 14 August 1862 at Mazomanie, James M. Bull enlisted him for three years, in Company E, 23rd Wisconsin. He mustered in 30 August 1862 at Madison. He was single, 30 years old, his home was Mazomanie, Wisconsin. He was a clerk at Brigadier Headquarters from 14 August 1863 and mail carrier April through December 1864. He mustered out with the company on 4 July 1865. They listed him as having deserted 2 February 1865, but on 9 March 1865 Robert M. Addison wrote a letter to reinstate Jacob whom they reported as a deserter. They explained that Jacob applied for transportation, but he failed to get it and while he was at New Orleans the regiment moved from White River, Arkansas to Helena, Arkansas. In 1889 he was living in Mount Jay, Pennsylvania, but he did not attend the 23rd Wisconsin's reunions in Madison in 1886 or 1889. In 1890 he was 61 years old, living in Sterling, Whitesides County, Illinois. He received a pension due to chronic rheumatism, disease of kidneys, chronic diarrhea and a deformity of his left foot. [132]

---

[131] Wisconsin Adjutant General, Regimental Descriptive Rolls 1861-1865; National Archives, Washington D.C., Pension File: Jacob C. Wikoff, Company E, 23rd Wisconsin Infantry invalid pension filed: 15 Sep 1890, application #939377, certificate #684287, filed in Illinois; 23rd Wisconsin, Company E; Civil War Unit Histories, Part 4, The Union- Midwest and West: Regimental Histories and Personal Narratives. *The Survivors of the Twenty-third Regiment Wisconsin Volunteer Infantry*, 1889.

Wood, Orestes Hawley

He was born 19 December 1829 in Austinburgh, Ohio, the son of Samuel Wood and Amy Welton. They named him for the Austinburg town doctor who delivered him and his twin, Erastus Austin Wood was named for the founder of Austinburg. He enlisted in Company A, 23rd Infantry, on 10 April 1863, rank Assistant Surgeon for three years. He mustered in 25 April 1863 at Plantation, Louisiana and mustered out on 4 July 1865. In September 1864 he requested a leave of absence for twenty days to provide suitable homes for his two young children. Since the death of their mother, they did not have a "parental protector" and since the death of their uncle, they had "no suitable home." He was commissioned Surgeon of the 51st Wisconsin, but that unit failed to meet the number of men needed for a surgeon. They raised only 444 men so they returned him to the 23rd Wiscosnin on 3 May 1865. He was present at the following engagements; Port Gibson, Champion Hills, Black River Bridge, Siege of Vicksburg, Mansfield, Jackson, Louisiana; Siege of Spanish Fort and Blakely, Alabama. In February 1857 they installed Dr. Wood as Worthy Chief Templar of Excelsior Lodge No. 36 in Richland Center, where they installed his wife as Worthy Vice Templar. Post 57, Grand Army of the Republic Department of Missouri, was named O. H. Wood, in Brookfield.

He married first Henrietta P. Canfield on 12 April 1854 at Auburn, Ohio. They moved with his parents to Richland Center where they had two children, Clark C. Wood born 1861 and Mary born 1862. His wife, Henrietta died there on 29 July 1862. A Lutheran minister at Fort Wayne married him, Indiana to Emily Fish Canfield. Emily was the widow of his wife's twin brother. Her former husband was Henry Canfield, who died at Sturgis, Michigan on 11 May 1864. Orestes died 1 March 1888, of injuries he received in a railroad accident at Brush Creek, Macon County, Missouri and is buried in the Brookfield Cemetery, Linn County, Missouri. In 1900 his widow, Emily stated that her net income did not exceed $250 per year. The only property she had was a two-story frame house and lot in the town of Austin, Illinois valued at $5,000. Her only income was from taking in boarders. [133]

---

[132] Wisconsin Adjutant General, Regimental Descriptive Rolls 1861-1865, 23rd Wisconsin, Field & Staff; National Archives, Washington D.C., Service Record & Pension File Emily Wood widow pension filed: 11 Mar 1892, application #544066, certificate #366532, filed in Illinois; Edward L. Woodyard of Armonk, New York, his

Great Grandfather is Eratus Austin Wood; Robert Kirkpatrick of Richfield, Minnesota, Great Grandfather is Erastus Austin Wood; History of Crawford & Richland County, Wisconsin (Springfield, IL, 1884) p. 1175; *Missouri - Our Civil War Heritage*, v.3, by the DUVCW, Julia Dent Grant, Tent #16, c1994, p.463-469.

Suggestions for Further Reading

An Historical Sketch of the 162nd Regiment NY Vol. Inf. (3d Metropolitan Guard), 19th Army Corps, 1862-1865. Albany, N.Y.: Weed, Parsons and Company, Printers, 1867.

Andrews, J. Cutler. *The North Reports the Civil War.* Pittsburgh: University of Pittsburgh Press, 1955.

Bankston, Marie Louise Benton. *Camp-Fire Stories of the Mississippi Valley Campaign.* New Orleans: L. Graham Co., Publishers, 1914.

Beecher, Harris H., M. D. *Record of the 114th Regiment New York State Volunteers.* Norwich, N.Y.: J. F. Hubbard, Jr., 1866.

Behlendorff, Maj. Frederick, USA. *The History of the Thirteenth Illinois Cavalry Regiment, Volunteers U.S. Army, from September, 1861 to September, 1865.* Grand Rapids, Mich.: Major, Lothar, Lippert, 1888.

Belisle, John G. *History of Sabine Parish Louisiana.* The Sabine Banner Press, 1912.

Bentley, Lt. W. H., USA. *History of the 77th Illinois Volunteer Infantry, Sept. 2, 1862-July 10, 1865.* Peoria, Ill.: Edward Hine, Printer, 1883.

Bering, John A., and Thomas Montgomery. *History of the Forty-Eighth Ohio Vet. Vol. Inf.* Hillsboro, Ohio: Highland News Office, 1880.

Boatner, Mark M.., III. *The Civil War Dictionary.* New York: Vintage Books, 1988.

Bringhurst, Thomas H., and Frank Swigart. *History of the Forty-Sixth Regiment Indiana Volunteer Infantry, September, 1861-September, 1865.* Logansport, Ind.: Wilson, Humphreys & Co., 1888.

Brooksher, William Riley. *War Along the Bayous. The 1864 Red River Campaign in Louisiana.* Brassey's, 1998.

Brown, Norman D., ed. *Journey to Pleasant Hill: The Civil War Letters of Captain Elijah P. Petty, Walker's Texas Division. CSA.* San Antonio: University of Texas Institute of Texan Cultures, 1982.

Bryner, Cloyd. *The Story of the Illinois 47th.* Springfield, Ill.: Philip Bros., Printer and Binders, 1905.

Culllum, Bvt. Maj.-Gen. George W. *Biographical Register of the Officers and Graduates of the U. S. Military Academy at West Point, N. Y.* Boston & New York, 1891

Faust, Patricia L., ed. *Historical Times Illustrated Encyclopedia of the Civil War.* New York: Harper & Row, Publishers, 1986.

Foote, Shelby. *The Civil War, a Narrative: Red River to Appomattox.* Vol. 3. New York: Random House, 1974.

Fowler, William M., Jr. *Under Two Flags: The American Navy in the Civil War.* New York: W.W. Norton & Company, 1990.

Gosnell, Lt. Comdr., H. Allen, USN. *Guns on the Western Waters: The Story of River Gunboats in the Civil War.* Baton Rouge: Louisiana State University Press, 1949.

Gould, Maj. John M., USV. *History of the First--Tenth-- Twenty-ninth Maine Regiments, in Service of the United States from May 3, 1861, to June 21, 1866.* Portland, Maine: Stephen Berry, 1871.

Harrington, Fred Harvey. *Fighting Politician: Major General N. P. Banks.* Westport, Conn.: Greenwood Press, Publishers, 1948.

Irwin, Richard B. *History of the Nineteenth Army Corps.* G. P. Putnam's Sons: New York, 1892.

Johnson, Ludwell H. *Red River Campaign: Politics & Cotton in the Civil War.* Kent, Ohio: Kent State University Press, 1993.

Jones, James P., and Edward F. Keuchel, eds. *Civil War Marine: A Diary of the Red River Expedition, 1864.* Washington: U.S. Government Printing Office, 1975.

Jones, Virgil Carrington. *The Civil War at Sea, July 1863- November 1865: The Final Effort.* Vol. 3. New York:: Holt, Rinehart and Winston, 1962.

Long, E. B., with Barbara Long. *The Civil War Day by Day: An Almanac 1861-1865.* New York: Da Capo Press, 1971.

Pinchon, Edgcumb. *Dan Sickles: Hero of Gettysburg and "Yankee King of Spain."* Garden City, 1945.

Porter, Adm. David D., USN. *The Naval History of the Civil War.* New York: Sherman Publishing Company, 1887.

Robertson, William Glenn. "Daniel E. Sickles and the Third Corps." in Gary Gallagher, ed. *The Second Day at Gettysburg*, Kent, 1993.

Sauers, Richard Allen. *A Caspian Sea of Ink: The Meade-Sickles Controversy."* Baltimore, 1989.

Stevenson, James. *History of the Excelsior or Sickles' Brigade.* Paterson, 1863.

Swanberg, W.A. *Sickles the Incredible*. New York, 1956.
The Union Army. Broadfoot Publishing Company: Wilmington, NC, 1998
Winters, John D. *The Civil War in Louisiana*. Louisiana State University Press, 1991.
Wisconsin Adjutant General, Regimental Descriptive Rolls 1861-1865.

Index

Addison, Albert C, 3
    Amelia Stuart, 2
    Ann Marie, 2
    Clarence Albert, 3
    Eliza H, 3
    Emily Robertine, 2
    Esther, 1
    Evelina L, 3
    George F., 3
    Harriet Matilda, 2
    John, 1
    Lillie H., 3
    Robert, 1
    Robert M, 5
    Robert Molford, 1, 2
    Stanley H., 3
Appleby, James, 103
    James Percy, 103
    John Francis, 103
    John Roy, 103
    Ruby Grace, 103
Armstrong, Fred J., 106
    James, 106
    Q. M. Capt, 21
Atkinson, Alexander, 107
    Grace Blanche, 107
    Lieutenant, 36, 95, 100-102
    Millie Bell, 107
Auertz, Catharine, 136
Ayers, Lieutenants, 44
Bainbridge, Mary E., 155
Baldwin, Lieutenant-Colonel, 42-43
Banks, Major-General, 12, 39
Barker, Susan M., 132
Barrus, Roxanna, 103
Bergholz, Sophia C., 120

Bering, Major, 43, 44
Black, Henry George
    Atkinson, 107
Brader, Lavina, 152
Bray, Harriet, 123
    Janey, 123
    William, 123
Bridgen, Major, 34, 52, 61
Brinton, Elizabeth Steinmetz, 142
Buel, Captain, 44
Buford, General, 92-94, 96, 99
    N. B., 95, 97, 99
    Napoleon Bonaparte, 109, 110
Bull, Captain, 51, 60-62, 65, 67, 70, 71, 75, 76, 77, 79, 80, 87, 90, 95
    James, 111
    James M, 5, 103, 111
    Lydia, 111
    T. H., 31
Burdett, Major, 44
Butler, Ann Maud, 112
    Christopher M., 112
    Edgar, 112
    James, 29
    James O, 112
    Mary Ann, 112
    Myra M., 112
Calkins, Anson, 113
    Franklin Welles, 113
    Jerome, 113
    Jerome Burton, 113
    John, 113
    John F., 61
    John Franklin, 113
    Stephen, 113

Cameron, General, 44,
    Robert Alexander, 115
Canby, General, 97
Canfield, Henrietta P, 172
    Henry, 172
Carey, William, 116
Carrion Crow Bayou, 9, 33
Cary, Sergerant, 91
Chatterton, Hannah H., 168
Chicago Mercantile Battery, 42, 44
Childs, Sarah, 109
Coats, Alvira, 168
Cone, Lieutenant, 42, 44
Cowan, Lieutenant-Colonel, 43
Crawford, Ruth, 113
Cresap, Daniel, 147
    Rebecca Ruth, 147
Dame, Hannah, 129
Dana, Napoleon Jackson Tecumseh, 118
Davidson, Major, 21
Davis, Colonel, 81, 82
Dawe, Hannah, 129
Day, Florence E., 160
DeGraff, Charles A, 6
Dennis, Elias Smith, 119
DeRussy, Fort, 56
Dickey, Captain, 42, 43
    Lieutenant, 70, 72, 120
Dickinson, Albert B, 120
    Arthur W, 120
    Benjamin, 120
    Emma C, 120
    Hattie E, 120
    Lula M,, 120
    Sady M, 120
    Sergeant, 87
Dillon, Charles H. , 134
Donaldson, Captain, 20
Drew, Arthur, 6
Dudley, Colonel, 40
Duncan, Agnes, 123
    Captain, 36, 101-102
    Elizabeth, 122
    Fred A, 123
    Jessie, 123
    John, 122
    John Elliott, 122
    Lieutenant, 100
    Paul, 123
    Ruth, 123
Dunham, Captain, 100
Dunlap, Mr., 138
Dussen, Adjutant, 101
Eads, James B, 13
Eberback, Nelson F., 137
Edward Walsh, 66
Eighty-third Ohio, 39, 40, 42, 43, 47
Eleventh Wisconsin, 25, 26
Ellet, Colonel Charles, 13
Emerson, Colonel, 43
Emory, William H, 11
Eugle, Greg, 71
Everett, William, 2, 6
Farland, Joseph John, 137
Fifth Wisconsin, 95
First Louisiana, 86, 89
First Wisconsin Battery, 53
Ford, Clayton E, 126
    Cornelius, 125
Fort Hudson, 18
Fort Jackson, 79
Fort Pillow, 16
Fort Powell, 76, 78, 79
Forts Henry, 14
Forty-eighth Ohio Infantry, 40, 41-44

Francis, Loren B, 99
Franklin, Major-General, 38, 41
Frisbie, Colonel, 81, 83
Frost, Donald K, 127
    Emma, 127
    Gertrude B, 127
    Julia Loretta, 127
    Lieutenant, 77, 85, 90, 100
    Louis D., 127
    Louis V,, 127
    Richard, 127
    Sarah, 127
Gainley, Fort, 75
George, Martha, 138
Gill, Alice M., 128
    Charles R., 65, 67, 128
    Martha A, 128
    Olive E., 128
Grange, Harriet J., 134
Granger, Major General Gordon, 74
Grant, General, 25, 66
Greene, Joseph E., 9, 129
    Major, 27, 30, 34, 36, 44, 60, 61, 67, 102
    William, 79, 80, 129
Greenwood, Mary Ann, 109
Guppy, Colonel, 59, 67
    John, 129
    Joshua James, 9, 129
Hancock, Colonel, 41
Harris, Alice, 131
    Anna Maria, 131
    Gilbert Tyson, 131
    Hannah, 131
    Hester, 131
    Lieutenants, 44
    Marian, 131
    Solomon, 131
Hatch, Lieutenant-Colonel, 44
Hayes, J. E., 48
Higbie, Lieutenant, 39, 44
Hill, Colonel, 98
    Edgar P., 9
Hindman, Prt, 53
Hoadley, Frank B, 106
Hodson, Harriet, 1
    John, 1
Hooker, Ellen, 126
Horton, James Everett, 132
    Sergeant, 87
Jane, Leslie M., 117
Jennie Rogers, 69
Jewett, Julia E, 166
Jolley, Mary L., 134
    Charles W., 134
    Frances D., 134
    James, 133
    John Lawlor, 133
    Lieut, 90, 100
Jones, Corporal, 86
    Jennette, 143
    John G, 135
Jussen, Alexander Shaler, 136
    Carl, 36, 136
    Edmund, 9
    Frederic Carl, 136
    Jacob, 136
    Katrina Ruetz, 136
    Mary Louise, 136
Kate Dale, 77, 78
Kellum, Mary A, 140
Kelly, Lydia, 117
Kendall, Laura Jane, 139
Ketterer, Mrs. Adele, 159

Kinsey, Alice Louise, 137
    Dr. John, 137
    Helen Fairchild, 137

    Lieutenant-Colonel, 81
    Virginia Elmira, 137
    William Baker, 137
Klauss, Captain, 44
Lancklon, Martha A., 128
Landram, Addie, 138
    Colonel, 37-39, 42, 43
    Ella, 138
    Katie, 138
    Lewis, 138
    Lieutenants, 44
    Mary, 138
    Walker, 138
    William Jennings, 138
Lawlor, Frances, 133
Lee, Ann, 1
    General, 37, 38, 40, 43
Lieber, Major, 39
Lincoln, McClellan, 93
Lindsey, Lieutenant-Colonel, 44
Loche, Mrs. Henry, 159
Longley, Sarah Ann, 155
Lucas, Gertrude Frost, 127
Lucas, Colonel, 40
Lull, Albert, 139
    Effie, 139
    Frank, 139
    Frank H., 139
    Harry, 139
    Henry, 139
    Lt. F. H, 51, 80
    Lt. L. H, 87

Lyle, 139
Mann, Major, 43
Marcy, Mary Ellen, 142
Marsh, Carlos E., 140
    Francis G., 140
    Freeman L., 140
    Lieutenant, 99, 100, 101
    Reuben F., 140
McClellan, George, 142
    George Brinton, 142
McCormack, Carroll, 143
    Charles, 143
    Howard, 143
McCormick, Lt., 72
McElwain, Bishop, 6
McFarland, Mr., 138
McGinnis, General, 67
    George Francis, 144
McGrew, Dr. J. S., 44
Mohr, Capt, 67
    Oscar, 145
Morrell, Henry H., 132
Mosley, Mrs. H. L., 165
Mott, S. H, 6
Murray, Margaret, 136
N. W. Thomas, 78, 87
Nelling, George, 73
Newell, Marshall, 103
Nineteenth Kentucky, 22, 33, 40, 42, 43
Ninety-second Colored Infantry, 83
Ninety-second U. S. Colored Infantry, 81
Ninety-ninth Illinois, 67
Ninety-seventh Illinois, 67
Ninety-sixth Ohio Infantry, 39, 40, 42, 43, 75
Noble, Captain, 100

Index   183

North, Captain, 68
    David, 145
Norton, John G, 146
    Lieutenant, 87, 99, 100
    Olivia C., 146
Ohio Belle, 86
One hundred and fourteenth New York, 47
One hundred and sixteenth New York, 49
One hundred and sixty-first New York, 40, 50, 54, 55, 57,73, 74, 75, 78, 81, 84, 86, 89
One hundred and thirtieth Illinois, 40, 42, 43
Ord, Edward Otho Cresap, 147
    James, 147
Parker, Charles H., 103
Parkin, Benjamin, 48, 149
Pierce, Lieutenant, 53
Pillow, General Gideon J., 16
Porter, David Dixon, 150
    John F., 150
    Rear Admiral, 53
Preston, George, 1
Prithard, Minerva A., 132
Propeller Tyler, 27
Prussia, Julich, 136
Quigley. Edney, 152
    Eva, 152
    George E., 152
    George W, 152
    John V., 152
    Sergeant, 87
    Vantile, 152
    William O., 152
R. B. Hamilton, 91

Ransom, Thomas Edward Greenfield, 23, 25, 26, 37, 41, 42, 44,15
Reed, Frank, 6
Reid, Major, 43
Reynolds, Edward, 155
    General, 91, 97
    Joseph Jones, 155
    Major General J. J., 99
Rice, Fanny, 156
    Gardiner, 156
    John S., 156
    Samuel G. , 61, 156
Richardson, Lieutenant, 44
Rickett, Emiline, 117
    John, 117
Ried, Elizabeth, 2
Roach, Martha, 159
Roberts, Hugh, 68, 158
    Sergeant, 29, 31
Roche, Clara J., 159
    Leon , 158
    Louis J., 159
    Robert G., 159
    Sergeant, 32, 67
Russell, Caroline, 139
Salter, Laura M, 137
Sanderson, Mrs. Thomas A., 165
Sanford, Martha Ann "Mattie" 111
Schlick, Agnes, 160
    Capt, 82
    Frank, 160
    Frank A, 160
    Jacob A., 160
    Nicholas, 160
    Volney, 160
Sears, Major, 44
Second Texas Cavalry, 70

Seventy-fifth Colored Infantry, 81, 83
Seventy-seventh Illinois, 1, 22, 40, 44, 75
Shaler, Alexander, 136
    Camilla J., 136
Sickles, Daniel Edgar, 161
Silver Wave, 74
Sixth Minnesota, 92, 95, 97, 99
Sixtieth Tennessee, 9
Sixtieth US Colored Infantry, 95, 99, 101
Sixty-seventh Indiana, 40, 43, 44, 75
Smith, Andrew Jackson, 163
    Elizabeth J., 106
    General A. J, 12., 45, 50, 51, 57
    Maj, 61
Soles, Nancy M., 170
Spicely, Colonel, 82
Spink, Anna Delight, 103
    Soloman Lewis, 103
Stanley, Lieutenant, 96, 100
Steamer Commerical, 90
Steamer Ellwood, 89
Steamer Florence, 91, 92
Steamer Ida Handy, 89
Steamer Kate Dale, 59
Steamer P. S. Swan, 15
Steamship Alliance, 27
Stone, Brigadier-General, 39, 43
    Gustavus, 103
Stucker, Kathern, 152
Sumner, Capt, 91
    James, 164
    Jane, 164
    John Douglas, 165
    John Milton, 164

Taylor, General Richard, 11, 12
Thirty-fifth Wisconsin, 72
Thirty-fourth Iowa, 75
Thompson, Mary Mercer, 148
Tilden, Ruth D, 123
Tolford, Arthur, 166
    Capt, 31, 61
    Frank, 166
    Joshua W. Jr. , 166
    Joshua Woodbury, 165
    Minnie, 166
    Ralph, 166
Transport Corrinthaun, 25
Transport Delaware, 92
Transport Rose Hamilton, 91
Tredway, Lieutenant, 44
Tucker, Mrs. Geo. S., 159
Twenty-first Iowa, 67
Tyler, John G. , 167
    Reginald, 167
Van Auden, Sarah M., 127
Vance, Colonel, J. W, 38
    Colonel, 43
Vilas, Captain, 44
    William F., 9
Walker, Sarah, 138
    William, 138
Ward, James Edward, 2
    William Allen, 2
Watson, Amelia, 167
Waugh, Jennie, 123
Webb, Amy, 169
    Clarence C., 169
    Clark, 168, 169
    Claude W., 169
    Corporal, 61
    Franklin, 168
    James, 168
Wells, Abigail, 113

Welton, Amy, 172
Wenzell, Ada Lelia, 137
    Samuel S., 137
West, Hannah, 156
    John, 156
    Mary Anne, 156
Wheeler, Ira H., 170
White, Captain P. H., 44
    Captain, 42, 44
Wikoff, Jacob C., 59, 48, 71, 77, 107, 171
Wilkinson, Job, 2
    Walter, 2
Williams, Charles H, 9
Wiltrout, Soloman, 61
Wisch, Anna, 158
Wishart, Jane, 103
Wood, Ella Amelia, 2
    Orestes Hawley, 172
    Samuel, 172
Woodward, Margaret, 137
    Mary, 165
Wright, Tempie, 107

www.ingramcontent.com/pod-product-compliance
Lightning Source LLC
Chambersburg PA
CBHW071423160426
43195CB00013B/1789